D1071997

LAST LEAVES

Stephen Leacock

LITERARY LAPSES
NONSENSE NOVELS
SUNSHINE SKETCHES
AFTERNOONS IN UTOPIA
MODEL MEMOIRS
TOO MUCH COLLEGE
THE BRITISH EMPIRE
MY REMARKABLE UNCLE
LAUGH WITH LEACOCK
STEPHEN LEACOCK'S LAUGH PARADE
HOW TO WRITE
HAPPY STORIES
LAST LEAVES

STEPHEN LEACOCK

LAST LEAVES

McCLELLAND & STEWART LIMITED
TORONTO, CANADA

* * * *

PRINTED IN CANADA.
WRIGLEY PRINTING COMPANY LIMITED
578 SEYMOUR STREET, VANCOUVER, B. C.

Acknowledgments

FOR their courtesy in permitting use of copyrighted material acknowledgment is made to: Oxford University Press, Canadian Branch, Toronto, for *All Right, Mr. Roosevelt*; The Canadian Bankers' Association, Toronto, for *Gold*; J. Walter Thompson Company, New York, for *To Every Child* which appeared in Pan American's FORUM OF THE FUTURE.

Preface

STEPHEN LEACOCK
(DECEMBER 30, 1869—MARCH 28, 1944)

By BARBARA NIMMO

THIS is not a biography of my uncle, Stephen Leacock. It is but a few of the things I have been thinking over recently that stand out in my memory during the years I knew him, especially when I lived in his house and did his secretarial work. It was a bit like living beside a volcano: there was nothing dull or routine in life. In the winter months we were in Montreal, in a comfortable town house at the foot of the mountain; in the summer as soon as McGill was over, or sooner if it could possibly be arranged, we were off to Orillia to his farm beside the lake.

The winter months were broken by many trips to all parts of the States for lectures—four or five a month—lecturing perhaps three or four times on each trip. Those who have heard Uncle Stephen lecture know there were few people who could hold an audience as he could; that there were few to equal him as a public speaker. "I started giving public humorous lectures to help the Belgian refugees in the last war, and went on after the war to help myself. My bread on the waters came back as cake. I lectured (1915-1937) all over the United States from Kansas City to the sea, and through England and Scotland, and in Canada from Halifax to Vancouver. To get a new audience I would have had to learn Chinese. So I stopped lecturing."

He was always nervous before each lecture; never could

eat; was not "fit company for any one" beforehand, as he told my father-in-law in Detroit where he'd gone to address some club. "See you afterwards, Harry." After a lecture was once over, he was at his best and funniest. He'd love to sit over a late supper, enthralling the guests with one story after another. He'd often drive up in a taxi—you'd hear him before the door was open—just off a night train, home from a successful trip. As he had his morning shave, he'd walk back and forth from the bathroom to his study, telling Stevie, his son, and me little bits of the trip. I was always nervous when I heard that taxi drive up for fear that perhaps I hadn't packed everything, or put that handkerchief in his dinner jacket pocket, or had forgotten that flask—no, I wouldn't have done that, for that headed the list.

He lectured at McGill three days a week, which gave him three free days for outside lectures and literary work. He'd started there under the reign of Queen Victoria (1901), giving just one lecture under her reign. He stayed on the staff there as head of the Department of Economics and Political Science from 1908 until his retirement in 1936. McGill was one of the great interests of his life and he one of the outstanding figures of McGill. You could always tell when he came into the Arts Building from his sure, heavy step and the loud thump of his cane on the marble floor, even if he didn't chance to pass any one and greet him in his deep, resonant voice. Students all spoke to him, and he always made a good pretence at knowing them even if he didn't.

He delighted in calling out as he walked through the halls, "Good morning, Gentleman," chuckling good-humouredly as half the student body turned in response. He was greeting his good and trusted friend Bill Gentleman, the head janitor of the Arts Building. Gentleman could always be relied on; he seemed to have an instinct or sixth sense for an important piece of mail—Uncle Stephen used the McGill address for all business mail. "My permanent address (in this world)," ne wrote to a business correspondent, "is McGill University, Montreal, as I was a professor there for thirty-six years and am now a Professor Emeritus."

In his sketch written at the death of Sir Arthur Currie, Principal of McGill and one of his close friends, he spoke of the lowly professors' following behind the various dignitaries of the business world and the military with "shabby, shuffling steps." I've never liked that bit of the eulogy, in other ways a splendid work, as it was really not what he thought of professors at all. He would rather have been a professor than anything else, and especially at McGill. He thought it a position of great respect, not humbleness. McGill he liked as a cosmopolitan seat of knowledge, not bound by religious sects or narrow policies. He liked the long months of leisure from set hours and routine which it gave: months he could devote to his writings and to life in the country. As he wrote somewhere, "In point of leisure, I enjoy more in the four corners of a single year than a business man knows in his whole life. I thus have what the business man can never enjoy, an ability to think, and, what is still better, to stop thinking altogether for months at a time."

He valued above all else "brains" and was quick to realize latent ability in his students. He did a great deal for many of his honour students, either getting them started out in the business world by sending them down to friends of his, heads of various large Canadian companies and themselves often old students of his, or urging them on to further degrees in outside colleges.

Of all his associates at the University, his closest friend was Professor René du Roure, head of the French Department, who died a few months after the collapse of France in this war, a tragedy which carried René away with it, brokenhearted at the fate of his dearly beloved France. The two had been friends for years, and I have often wished that I could have imbibed more from their lengthy conversations

and arguments on wars, history, literature and education.
They were a brilliant pair. They played a great deal of chess
together in the evenings in my uncle's study and on days
when he lectured in the afternoon they invariably met for
a game of billiards at the University Club. Their matches
were famous around the Club, not for the excellence of their
game but for the fun and good humour they had over it.
They played for a dollar a game, and the same dollar changed
hands back and forth as the handicap favoured first one and
then the other. I could always tell who had won for the afternoon, as on a snowy winter's eve they'd get out of their taxi,
laughing wholeheartedly because the loser of the day paid
the fare. They'd have a drink of sherry together before René
would start off around the corner to his apartment.

Uncle Stephen had, during his thirty-six years on the staff,
given up much time and thought to the direction of the
Arts Faculty, as a dominant voice on the faculty committee.
He never wanted to be principal or dean of a faculty but just
the head of the department, with few administrative duties
to perform. What duties of this nature there were he could
do in a minute with a pen and a piece of Bristol board,
plotting a course or a timetable for lectures. He had a quick
and orderly mind in planning things. I remember the first
Bristol board table I saw of his when, as a little girl, I gazed
at the neat charts he'd made for some medicine Stevie was
taking. After that, when I came to stay, we used sheets and
sheets of it each week in the study and at McGill; there
was a large chart that hung behind the study door for lecture
engagements, and others for expenses, for household routine,
etc. In the barnyard at Orillia, too, hung charts on the
amount of grain the livestock got a day, the rotation to weed
the garden, and each of the hired men's duties.

When, with the enforcement of the sixty-five age limit,
he was asked to retire in 1936, he made no pretence about
liking it. He wanted to go right on lecturing—it gave him
just enough of a routine to fit the rest of his work around,

a sort of "stay," as it were. His disappointment led to quite a bitter feeling for some time against the University he had served so well. "I was then (1936) retired, much against my will, on grounds of senility, having passed the age of sixty-five."

In the fall of 1936 an invitation came to go across Canada on a lecture tour. He had never lectured in Canada for money; he had spoken at numerous clubs and societies but either for nothing or for charitable proceeds, as when he lectured during the First World War for the benefit of the Belgian Relief. There followed several weeks of breathless planning, arranging lectures in the various cities and frantic packing, until the night of November 25th when Uncle Stephen and Stevie got off with two huge black suitcases plastered with bright red stars for "quick identification." His letters came back full of enthusiasm over the trip. "The success of my trip has been overwhelming. More than one could have imagined." (Edmonton, December 13.) In Winnipeg he wrote, "It is just like a come-to-Jesus parade. I talked at the Fort Gary Hotel and a little before the meeting they said, 'This is the record for seats except for the Queen of Rumania,' and a little later, 'This beats the Queen of Rumania,' and later, 'The Queen is nowhere.' " And again from Victoria, "I had the most marvellous success here with a talk yesterday on *Economic Separatism in the Empire*. They laughed and cried, just about: never was there anything like it, they said. I put a lot of work into each speech and never a note." But with all his enthusiasm was a determination never to lecture again. "No more this season, and please God I won't need to lecture any more—wonderful success—all records broken, but it's too hard." I was told to answer letters for lecture engagements, regretting that "Professor Leacock is in the West but has asked me to say that he cannot take on any further engagements at present."

"Don't say *never*; I might have to. But I mean *never* to, never, never; I am tired but I can finish this and then I am done. Except for my book, I'll never work again, never; I'll

write if I want to." And lecture again, except to small gath-
erings of Ontario Conservatives or McGill Alumni rallies,
he never did, but his writing never stopped. He arrived back
and immediately started off on *My Discovery of the West*
while "the iron was hot."

$$\cdot \qquad \cdot \qquad \cdot \qquad \cdot \qquad \cdot \qquad \cdot \qquad \cdot$$

I have never heard people laugh as they did around his
dining room table and I never expect to hear people laugh
like that again. He loved entertaining and almost always
made some visiting celebrity an excuse for a party—an author,
actor, or explorer. (He was always fascinated with explorers.
He nearly went on an expedition to the South Pole with
Shackleton or Vilhjalmur Stefansson—I have forgotten which
one it was. He knew them both but when he found he could
not take along his own supply of whiskey, the long cold nights
of the sub-arctic seemed too much.)

So many famous and interesting people have been gathered together in the Côte des Neiges house or have been
asked for dinner or supper at the University Club. At home
we'd have cocktails first in his study upstairs, an attractive
book-lined room, books clear to the ceiling, a large window all
across one side of the room, giving a beautiful view down
over the city and the harbour he loved. He was seldom in
his dinner jacket and ready when the guests arrived—never
before the first few, as he finished up some letters or went
over a bit of MS. He liked to plan the meal himself, pre-
ferring a French type of dinner with many courses. He often
made little menus by longhand for each guest, so they
wouldn't get "a knockout blow when they came to the *pièce
de résistance.*"

One winter, I think it must have been in 1934, he gave a
series of radio talks, short bits from his humorous writings.
It was the first time any one had been able to persuade him
to talk over the radio—he didn't like it; said he was afraid
of the new technique. There were some sixteen broadcasts
in all, every Tuesday and Friday night for fifteen minutes

around ten o'clock. His friends in Montreal enjoyed these evenings, for in order to have "some one" to talk to and not a piece of metal, he'd ask a dozen or more friends to join him for drinks at the Club and then go in a body over to the broadcasting studio. After the talk was over, the fun of the evening came, as we all piled into taxis and drove on up to the house for a gay supper party, full of fun and good cheer, with Uncle Stephen's spontaneous, jovial wit to set a merry pace. But he still didn't like giving radio addresses and never did again except when a speech before a large audience was put on the air—he didn't need to think of the microphone then. He needed to feel the pulse of his audience, for what he describes of Dickens in his book on his life I think was true, very true, of his own public speaking. "Dickens's audiences were quite truly carried away. They were outside themselves. They laughed and they sobbed; they were in an 'ecstasy.' And Dickens controlled them with hand and voice and eye—like a magician."

He always read aloud his articles or his books, piece by piece, to any of us who happened to be around. There was a sort of exultation in his spirits then, as over a thing well done. "Fetch me that MS. on my study table," he would ask me (I'd usually find it somewhere else), "and my spectacles—I don't know where." So many of his stories I've heard him read as he stood before the fire either in the living room in the Orillia house or in his study in Montreal. I can always hear his rich and full-toned voice as I read anything he has written. I can hear the laughter that went with it; can feel the pauses of emphasis. I remember especially well the night he read *My Remarkable Uncle* to us. A group of my young friends were gathered that evening around the fire. Uncle Stephen appeared about midnight, clad in dressing gown and slippers and smoking a pipe, after two or three hours of sleep. He liked going off to bed early, often just after dinner, with his book and spectacles—to reappear a few hours later if there was any one still up to talk to; if not, he'd cut himself a hunk

of cheese and crackers at the sideboard and go off to bed
again.

He wrote in the early morning, often (especially in Montreal) being up and at his desk in the early hours when I
arrived home from a very late party. If he couldn't write on
a new book or article, there were always letters to answer,
plans for the farm to draw up, outlines for McGill work,
some treatise or other that he could work on until at another
time his mind, rested and refreshed, was ready for something
"real." He had a habit of "putting things in writing"—a discussion on some college course, a talk he'd had with the Dean
on some student's work, a confirmation of a conversation
with a storekeeper. Perhaps all this because he hated the tele-
phone, whenever possible having others take the message. It
took time to train a maid to say, "No, Mr. Leacock is not in,"
and yet not muff up some important business call.

.   .   .   .

The summers, as I have said, were spent in Orillia at his
country house there, Old Brewery Bay. He used to say he'd
judge his visitors by that name. "If they like the name Old
Brewery Bay, they're all right. They can have everything on
the place. I have known that name, the Old Brewery Bay, to
make people feel thirsty by correspondence as far away as
Nevada." The house there was large and comfortable with
a wide-swept lawn to the lake. Two large furnaces made it
habitable in winter, and up to a few years ago he would come
there with a number of friends and his family for a gay and
bright Christmas holiday. With the war and the consequent
shortage of domestic help and the difficulty in getting all
kinds of work done around a house, the place had begun to
show the need for repairs and paint and refixing. But Uncle
Stephen seemed hardly to notice all that. He reminded me
to some small degree of old E. P. Leacock, whom he describes in one of the best sketches he ever wrote, *My Remarkable Uncle*. Not that Uncle Stephen was the likable
humbug that E.P. was, but he had the vision to see the beau-

tiful about him and not the ugly; the possibility of what things might be and not what they really were. He'd direct us, full of kind welcome, to the "west wing" bedrooms when I arrived for the summer vacation with my husband and little girl. The room faced the west, yes, but there were no screens and there wasn't a stopper to the bath. And it really did not matter.

Life in Orillia all took place within the bounds of the Old Brewery Bay, except for an occasional trip to a trout stream or out fishing in his old sailing boat. He has written so many charming stories of the great delights of fishing, and as I myself know nothing about fishing, I leave that part out—except to say that Uncle Stephen's enthusiasm carried over to any one that had never liked to fish before. I think he enjoyed a fishing companion who didn't know *too* much. Then he had the fun of showing how it was done. He'd finish in his study in the early forenoon on a nice day and then go off for a fishing trip, full of enthusiasm. There was always a lunch to be packed to take aboard, with drinks and sandwiches. There was a standard list to be made up and stowed away in solid boxes constructed so you could stand on them in the boat without breaking things. Everything else stopped in the routine of farm and house while these trips set off: some one packed the lunch, another bicycled to town for worms, and another fixed the boat. There were trappings and devices on that boat which were unique in sailing annals and which Uncle Stephen had thought up to make life aboard the small dinghy as easy and leisurely as possible. I remember once in the hustle and bustle of getting Uncle Stephen and a friend off, he called out to the young hired man of the hour, "Bring me a piece of ice, a small piece about the size of your brain." And he chuckled as the boy returned with a chunk as big as a large ten gallon hat. I remember another day as I went to the boathouse to see if I could sight the returning boat, the better to time the dinner hour, I found the fishermen just about to dock in a dead calm. Uncle Stephen was at the

rudder, watch in hand, and his younger companion pulling
hard at the oars. "Just on time, just on the dot," shouted
Uncle Stephen.

Gardening and farming came even before fishing. I suppose
you might call the farm a truck farm. Tomatoes, beans and
peas he raised in quantity to sell to the village store, and at
different times other things were tried out. One summer it
was Montreal melons, which reached a size of twenty pounds
but needed as much care as a new-born baby; another year,
turkeys. I remember our dining one Thanksgiving on the sole
survivor of a brood of one hundred which, at fifty cents to
start plus the feed (until one by one they died), represented a
hundred dollars. But Uncle Stephen could always laugh it off,
very literally, as he'd often write an amusing story and make
many hundreds more. He spoke of his place in a letter: "I
have a large country house—a sort of farm which I carry on
as a hobby . . . Ten years ago the deficit on my farm was
about a hundred dollars; but by well-designed capital expenditure, by drainage and by greater attention to details, I have
got it into the thousands."

Gardening and farming were not the only things that went
on around the farm. There was always something in the process of being made—a henhouse or boathouse, cottage or lodge.
Uncle Stephen designed them all himself. The barnyard he
made for fun like an old French stockade, a high green fence
with a building at each of the four corners for feed, tools and
chickens, etc., with the stable for one work horse and two
cows in the centre. There was a charming little lodge, a cottage by the lake, and a boathouse on the bay. The only trouble was that once he had finished, Uncle Stephen was liable
to lose interest in them—might even start ripping one apart
to start another. But it was all fun, anyway.

He liked entertaining in Orillia particularly, to fill the
house with week-end guests, friends from everywhere. He
liked to look down the broad table and proudly point out
that everything was "off the farm," except the can of sardines

in the hors d'oeuvres. He might acknowledge that it could have been done cheaper (if one included "capital cost and labour"), very much cheaper, by a caterer up from Toronto, but that wasn't the point. On a summer evening if the crowd were large, we might dine on the sun gallery which he would suddenly turn into a fairy bower of green by having vast ferns brought in from the surrounding woods and stuck in huge pots. Once he even had flowers cut from the back garden and stuck all along the perennial beds to give a bit of color when the blossoms there were off season. He was often a hard taskmaster; he worked hard and energetically himself and expected it of others. I've known him to fire all the maids with a houseful of guests and hire them back the next day at increased pay.

He'd write me after I was married and had gone away: "I find that from May 1st to May 15th we served 333 meals, and they cost 17 cents each for outside supplies, but as many things represent 'stocking up' (having just come up from Montreal) and as inside supplies increase greatly with broilers and vegetables, I hope to get down to close to 10 cents . . . The fowls, eating by the measured pound of food of which I know the cost, are running at about a little over $15 a month; but the hens lay not far from 50 cents a day (20 cents a day cash and the rest we eat), so that the hens are very nearly feeding the 225 broilers." He enjoyed getting things like this down on paper—farm accounts, household accounts; called it "putting the college to it"—then he'd forget it all the next day.

He never learned to drive a car and knew nothing about a car except, as he often said, that it needed gasoline. "How's the gas supply?" he'd always ask a parting guest. As long as a person had a licence, that was all Uncle Stephen asked about their driving. However, the rule of the road when you drove for Uncle Stephen was to "get her up to thirty-five and hold her there." I've had many a trip between Montreal and Orillia at that speed—the difficulty was to keep the chauffeur awake.

I remember once Uncle Stephen was fined nineteen dollars for allowing his truck to be driven without flares. He showed up the fallibility of the law in a letter he wrote accompanying the check, with a twist of humour to bring out his point. He could do this sort of thing well; it was hard to come up against him in an argument. "I desire to say that I am fined because I permitted my driver to drive my truck without flares. I never in my life heard of flares until now; neither did my driver, and I had no notion that a truck must carry flares—nobody told me. There is no obligation on the man who sold me the truck to tell me about flares, and there ought to be, but there isn't. Now what comes next? There may be a dozen more obligations and limitations. My driver speaks French. Shall I be fined in Ontario for that? My truck is painted green. Is that legal? Or is it too Irish?"

No article about Uncle Stephen ever omits a description of his personal appearance. He was a rugged, fine-looking man, not really large as most people make him out to be, but with a large head, tremendous stride and a deep, rich voice—all of which made him seem bigger than he really was. He had deep-set, keen blue eyes with a constant sparkle, just sometimes lit up by a flash of rage. His hair, and he had plenty of it, covered his head thickly and crept down his forehead in a fetlock not easily kept brushed down. I remember my grandmother's once remarking how grey his hair was getting. "That's just because I have some left—you don't notice the other boys."

To my knowledge he had never been near his King Street tailor in seventeen years, yet he got two suits a year made to order by measurements that were designed for comfort rather than style. Huge, loose coats, long in the sleeve and body, and wide trousers. They came in a salt-and-pepper cloth, blue worsted, and Oxford grey. I remember once when the cloth samples arrived we picked one out—a nice grey with a bit of blue in the two-inch sample—which turned out to be the inside of a large panel plaid. It was easy to shop for him—

which I always did. His shirts were blue or white broadcloth
in a 17″ collar, when a 15½″ one would have been a good
fit; heavy black lisle socks; navy blue and white polka dot ties,
the only variation in the size of the dot. He sometimes
shopped for his hats and his shoes, but if time ran out, that
was easily done by taking the soft grey fedora or the black
laced boot down for a "repeat order." In the evening (and he
enjoyed dressing for dinner if only one or two people were
coming to dine), he wore a loose fitting dinner jacket and
trousers, with a dress shirt pleated and done up down the
front. (He wouldn't stand for any of these "newfangled"
shirts—"just stiff bibs, fake!") With this went a straight narrow black tie in a loose bow.

．　　　．　　　．　　　．　　　．　　　．　　　．

I could go on writing indefinitely of little happenings that
I remember, for each day was full of incident and interest.
There was his early life on the farm; his days at Upper Canada
College; at Toronto University. He then went as a housemas-
ter to Upper Canada College: "the most dreary, the most
thankless, and the worst paid profession in the world." Then
to Chicago to take his Ph.D., and afterwards to McGill as a
lecturer. His lecture trips to England, around the Empire on
the Rhodes Trust Foundation, all this went to make a full
and busy life. He worked hard and unsparingly, writing in
all over fifty books, touching on a vast number of subjects.
He had definite and well-found views on all questions,
thought deeply on the welfare of mankind. If the world could
grow rich and still pay for the horrors of modern warfare,
then with the peace there should be a way to run things so
that there could be more than enough for every one. This he
went on to discuss in some of his more recent articles.

His letters alone to his many friends, students and business
acquaintances could fill volumes, for he wrote easily and rapidly. He was quick to write to any one to congratulate him on
a new achievement or to send a sympathetic note on a be-
reavement. He wrote me when my little girl was a baby:

"Stevie has been interested every minute about the baby, as I have, but he never writes, is too young to realize that people want to hear. Nowadays if the Queen had a baby I'd write: 'Dear Queen, this is great news'—but young people don't understand that."

I have gathered together here various articles that he had recently written for magazines and newspapers. They quite naturally fall into groups: a number of humorous articles, such as *"Living with Murder," "Are Witty Women Attractive to Men?"*; several which deal in a light vein with a ponderous question, such as *"Common Sense and the Universe"*; two appraisals of English humourists, Lewis Carroll and W. S. Gilbert; and, in particular, a number on the world after the war.

Contents

LAST LEAVES

I

AMONG THE ARTICLES AND ESSAYS COLLECTED HERE IN
"LAST LEAVES" ARE A GROUP OF HUMOROUS SELECTIONS
WHICH STEPHEN LEACOCK WROTE FOR THE MOST PART
DURING THE LAST YEAR, SINCE THE PUBLICATION OF HIS
BOOK OF SIMILAR SKETCHES, "HAPPY STORIES, JUST TO
LAUGH AT."

Are Witty Women Attractive to Men?

SLAVES murmur to one another in their chains. They whisper what they think of their masters. In the same way the generality of men, being enslaved by women, whisper, when in safety, what they think. Slave No. 1 in his Club murmurs to Slave No. 2 that women have no sense of humour. Slave No. 2 agrees, and Slave No. 3, overhearing from his armchair, says quite boldly, "They certainly have not." After which quite a colloquy ensues among the slaves. But when the wife of Slave No. 1 asks at dinner what was the talk at the Club, he answers, "Oh, nothing much." Yet his inmost feeling is that women have no sense of humour, and if a woman is witty, she has somehow come by it wrongly. He daren't speak right out, but I will speak for him.

Having been asked to answer the question, "Are witty women attractive to men," I answer decidedly, "No." Having said this I dodge behind the Editor and explain it.

There are, of course, a lot of immediate qualifications to be made to it. In the first place, are witty people in general attractive to anybody? Not as a rule. They get tiresome. It is terribly hard to be witty without getting conceited about it. I used to be very witty myself, till I learned to be careful about it. People don't like it. There are two things in ordinary conversation which ordinary people dislike—information and wit. Most people—most men at any rate—like to gather up information out of the *Digests*, which are the passion of the hour. But they won't take it from you. You're not a *Digest*. So, too, with wit. They've learned by experience that if they laugh at one thing, they'll have to go on. . . . So if this applies to men with men, it applies all the more to men with women. Luckily women don't go in for information; or if they give it, it is so incorrect as to be harmless.

In the next place, it goes without saying that some witty women are attractive to some men. This, by a happy disposition of providence, happens to all kinds of women, like attracting unlike. Hence witty women always have silent husbands. That's why they got married. There is a particularly decent type of man who finds it restful not to have to talk. When, in his youth, he meets a girl who talks all the time, that exactly suits him. He doesn't have to say anything. Ten years later you'll see them enter a drawing room together. The host says to the man, "Looks like an early winter," and he answers, "Certainly does!" The host says, "Have a cocktail," and he answers, "Certainly will." By that time his wife has started in on the conversation; he doesn't have to talk any more. People commonly call this type an adoring husband. He isn't. His wife is just a sort of fire screen. The real adoring husband overtalks his wife, overdominates her, pays with unexpected presents for easy forgiveness of his ill temper, and never knows that he adored her till it is too late, because now she cannot hear it. . . .

We will add another qualification, that one reason why some men don't care for the society of witty women is because of their own egotism. They want to be *it*. A wise woman sitting down to talk beside such a man will not try to be witty. She will say, "I suppose you're just as busy as ever!"

All men, you see, have the idea that they are always busy, and if they are not, a woman can soon persuade them that they are. Just say, "I don't see how you do it all," without saying what all is.

Another very good opening for women sufficiently self-possessed is to say, "Well, I hear you are to be congratulated again!" You see there is always something; either the office staff gave him a stick last month, or the Rotary Club elected him an Elder Brother. He'll find something. If he doesn't, then say to him that if he hasn't heard of it yet, you are certainly not going to tell. Then don't see him for a month, till the Fireman's Benevolent Union has elected him an Honorary Ash Can. He'll get something if you wait.

So you see there are ever so many ways for women to make a hit without trying to be witty.

Nor have women, themselves, any particular use for witty men. Instinctively they admire courage, though unhappily courage often goes with brutality and savagery. In the next degree they admire the courage of character of strong people on whom one can rely. But intellect comes last. Unhappily, women also have their superficial admirations, things they *fall for*—it's too bad, but they do. Women are apt to fall for a poet, for anything with long hair and a reputation. Round him they cluster, searching his thoughts. He probably hasn't got any. But wit, in all the procession, comes last, with only a cap and bells behind it.

Another thing is this. By this very restriction of their province of humour, women are saved from some of the silly stuff that affects the conversation of men. Take puns. They have pretty well died out now. The last of the punsters is probably dead, or in hiding. But many of us can still remember the social nuisance of the inveterate punster. This man followed conversation as a shark follows a ship, or, to shift the simile, he was like Jack Horner and stuck in his thumb to pull out a pun. Women never make puns; never did; they think them silly. Perhaps they can't make them—I hope not.

Nor have women that unhappy passion for repeating funny stories in order to make a hit, which becomes a sort of mental obsession with many men. The "funny story" is a queer thing in our American life. I think it must have begun on the porch of the Kentucky store where they whittled sticks all day. At any rate, it has become a kind of institution. It is now a convention that all speakers at banquets must begin with a funny story. I am quite sure that if the Archbishop of Canterbury were invited to address the Episcopal Church of America, the senior bishop would introduce him with a

story about an old darky, and the Archbishop would rise to
reply with a story about a commercial traveller. These stories
run riot in our social life and often turn what might be a
pleasant dinner into an agonized competition, punctuated
with ruminating silence. Women keep away from this. They
like talk about people, preferably about themselves, or else
about their children, with their husband as a poor third, and
Winston Churchill competing with Mrs. Chiang Kai-shek for
fourth place. It may not be funny but it's better than darkies
and commercial travellers. . . .

There is also the most obvious qualification to be made in
regard to women's sense of humour in general and women's
wit in particular, that of course individual exceptions, however conspicuous, do not set aside the general rule. There is
no doubt that at least one of the most brilliant humourists of
the hour in America is a woman. Many would say, *the* most
brilliant. Such a faculty for reproducing by simple transcrip-
tion the humour of social dialogue has, it seems to me, never
been surpassed. But one swallow doesn't make a summer,
though one drop of ink may make all humour kin.

The truth is that the ideal of ordinary men is not a witty
woman, but *a sweet woman*. I know how dangerous the term
is, how easily derided. Sweetness may easily cloy into sugari-
ness, or evaporate into saintliness. A saint with hair parted in
the middle, with eyes uplifted, may be all right for looking
out from the golden bars of heaven, but not so good for the
cocktail bars below.

And yet, I don't know. A saint can kick in sideways anywhere.

It might easily be objected that all such opinions about
sweetness in women are just left-over Victorianism, half a
century out of date. Witty women, it will be said, may have
seemed out of date in the stodgy days of women's servitude,
but not now. The men and women of today—or call them
the boys and girls—mix on an entirely different plane. All the
old hoodoos and taboos are gone. All the girls smoke. They

use language just as bad as any the men care to use. They drink cocktails and give the weaker men the cherry. In other words, they can curse and swear and drink—they're real comrades. In point of physique, they may not be equal to the men but after all they can drive a car and fly a plane and telemark all over hell on skis—what more do you want?

So why shouldn't a girl of that type, the new girl who has conquered the world, be witty if she wants to? What more charming than a witty girl, half-stewed, as compared with a girl half-stewed and silent as a toad full of gravel?

To all of which I answer, "No, no, it's just an illusion!" There are no new girls, no new women. Your grandmother was a devil of a clip half a century before you were born. You telemark on skis; she cut ice in a cutter. You only knew her when she was wrinkled and hobbling, reading the Epistle to the Thessalonians in a lace cap and saying she didn't know what the world was coming to. The young have always been young, and the old always old . . . men and women don't change. It took thousands, uncounted thousands, of years to make them what they are. The changes that you think you see lie just on the surface. You could wash them away with soap and hot water.

But now I'll tell you another thing. All this new era of ours of emancipated women, and women in offices and women the same as men, is just a passing phase, and the end of it is already in sight. A great social disaster fell on the world. The industrial age built up great cities where people lived, crowded into little boxes, where there was no room for children, where women's work vanished because they were dispossessed, where national population was kept going by additions from God knows where, and national safety was jeopardized by the increasing scarcity of our own people. . . . We had a close shave of it.

Then came the war in the air. . . . It has bombed the industrial city out of future existence. They know that already in England. The bomb is decentralizing industry, spreading the population out. They will never go back. This will mean different kinds of homes, homes half-town, half-country, with every man his acre. . . . Every one's dream for a little place in the country, a place to call one's own, will come true. Socialized up to the neck, the individual will have its own again under his feet.

And the children? There must be four or five for every marriage. It is the only path of national safety, safety by the strength and power of our kin and kind, bred in our common thought and speech and ideal. Without our own children, the wave of outside brutes from an unredeemed world will kill us all. Later, we can redeem the world but we must save ourselves first. . . . Everybody will know that. In re-organized society the nation's children will be the first need, the main expense of government. Women who see to that need see to nothing else. . . . That will be done in the home, for there will be no paid domestic service except contract labour by the hour from the outside, labour as good as ladyship, wearing a gold wrist watch and a domestic college degree. . . . But the main thing will be the home and behind it the long garden and trim grass and flower and vegetable beds, and father trying to plant a cherry tree from a book.

When England has been bombed into the country, America will follow. Our cities will go, too. . . . No one will *live* in New York any more than miners live in a coal mine.

So the world will be all different. One little century will do it. Even half a century will show the full outline of it. Surviving on . . . surviving on into this altered world will be the queerest old set of left-over creatures, as queer as our left-over Victorians, only queerer. These old women will be happy and alert and self-assertive, but they will still not know how to fry an egg or repeat a nursery rhyme, for they only had three-quarters of a child each. . . . The boys and girls of twenty will think them very funny. . . . But my! Won't they be witty when they get together and cackle.

So that, you see, is why I don't think witty women are attractive to men. You don't see the connection? Well, perhaps you remember Molière's play called *The Doctor by Accident* (*Le Médecin Malgré Lui*) where the supposed doctor, called in to diagnose a case, gets off a vast rigmarole about nothing in particular and adds at the end, ". . . and that is why your daughter has lost her speech." You see, he didn't know anything about it.

Possibly it was like that.

Living with Murder

I AM a great reader of detective fiction. That is, I have been up to now, but I see I shall have to give it up. It begins to affect one's daily life too much. I am always expecting something sudden, something sensational, to happen, such as that a criminal will "burst around the corner" on the run and I shall immediately have to "time" his burst.

They always *time* everything in the stories, so as to have it ready for the evidence.

That is why I now find myself perpetually "timing" myself all day, so that I can swear to everything.

For instance, I went down to dine three or four days ago with my old friend Jimmy Douglas at his house. He lives alone. This, by itself, would make any reader of crime fiction *time* him. I paused a moment at the lighted doorway before ringing the bell and noted that my watch said 7:00 P.M. A street clock just visible down the street, however, marked 7:02½ P.M. Allowing for the fact that my watch was one minute slow, I was thus able to place the time fairly accurately as at 7:01¼.

What did I do that for? Well, don't you see—what if I rang the bell, received no answer, and at length pushed the door open (it would yield quite easily) to find Jimmy Douglas lying prone in the doorway? That would settle the time, wouldn't it? And what if he were still warm (he would be, good fellow)? That would settle just how warm he was.

So I rang the bell. The Chinese servant who answered the door showed me noiselessly into the lighted sitting room and motioned me to sit down. The room was *apparently* empty. I say *apparently*, because in the stories you never know. If

Douglas's body was lying hunched up in a corner (you know the way they hunch them up), my business was to take care to look up in the air, around the room, everywhere except in the right place to see him.

I did this and I noticed that there was an Ormolu clock on the mantel (there always is) and that it stood at 7:04 P.M., practically corroborating my previous estimate.

I was just checking it over when Douglas came in.

I noticed his manner at once and could only describe it as extremely normal, even quiet, certainly, I would say, free from any exhilaration. Whether this was a first effect of arsenic poisoning, or just from seeing me, I am not prepared to state.

We had a cocktail. Douglas left two distinct fingerprints on the glass. I held mine by the rim.

We sat down to dinner at 7:30 P.M. Of this I am practically certain because I remember that Douglas said, "Well, it's half-past," and as he said it the Ormolu clock chimed the half-hour. A further corroboration is that the Chinese servant entered at that moment and said, "Half-past seven!" I gather, therefore, that the hour was either seven-thirty or possibly a little before or a little after.

At any rate—not to make too much of details—we sat down to dinner. I noticed that at dinner Douglas took no soup. I attached no importance to this at the time, so as to keep it for afterwards. But I also took care on my part to take no fish. This, of course, in the event of arsenic poison would at least, by elimination, give a certain indication of how the poison had been administered. Up to this point the Chinese servant's manner was quite normal, in fact, Chinese.

I am not able to say whether Douglas took coffee after dinner; I slipped up there. I had got talking, I remember, of my views on Allied Strategy and for the moment forgot not only to time him but to notice what he ate. This makes an unfortunate gap in the record.

However, Douglas, I noticed, seemed but little inclined to

talk after dinner. I was still unfolding to him my views on
Allied Strategy in the war, but he seemed unable to listen
without signs of drowsiness. This obviously might be due to
arsenic poisoning.

I left at nine, having noticed that Douglas roused up with
a slight start as the Ormolu clock struck, and said, "Nine!
I thought . . . I thought it was ten."

I drove home in a taxi; and can easily identify the taxi,
even if abandoned in a stone quarry, by a mark I made in the
leather. I can identify the taxi man by a peculiar scar.

That, as I say, was three days ago. I open the newspaper
every morning with a nervous hand, looking for the finding
of Douglas's body. They don't seem to have found it yet. Of
course I don't know that he lost it. But then it is never known
that a body is lost until some one finds it.

One thing is certain, however. I am all ready if they
do. . . . If any news comes out I can act at once. I have the
taxi man, and the fingerprints and the Ormolu clock—that's
all you need usually.

What Can Izaak Walton Teach Us?

EVERYBODY—or at least everybody who goes fishing, and the rest don't count—knows the name of Izaak Walton. Many of them would also remember that he was called the Father of Angling and that he wrote a book called *The Compleat Angler*. This is acknowledged to be one of the world's books. Only the trouble is that the world doesn't read its books, it borrows a detective story instead.

So it may not be without interest to outdoor people—anglers, men of the bush and streams and such—to turn over again the pages of the old volume and see what Izaak Walton can teach us. This, especially, if we can catch something of the leisurely procedure, the old-time courtesy and, so to speak, the charming tediousness of people with lots of time, now lost in our distracted world.

Izaak Walton, let us pretend to remember, was born in the reign of Queen Elizabeth (1593) but lived so long and so peacefully—old fishermen never die; they merely fade away—that he only passed away at the age of ninety at the end of the Stuart period. People reading *The Compleat Angler* would take him for a country gentleman. But he wasn't. Indeed, in the phrase of the times he wasn't a gentleman at all. He came to London from the little town of Stafford and in London he kept an ironmonger's shop in the very heart of the city. It was so small a place that there was hardly room to turn around in, certainly not with a fishing rod, for it was only six feet by seven feet six inches.

But it must have been a grand little place from which to dream of the woods and meadows around Stafford and to let the noise of the city die on his ear till he could catch the murmur of the babbling streams. . . . Thus you may see to-day, if you have the eye for it, many an imprisoned, incomplete angler working at a desk with the sound of a waterfall in his ears, or selling across a sporting goods counter the tackle that he never has the good fortune to use.

Walton says that fishermen are the Lord's own people, and no doubt he's right. "The primitive Christians," he remarks, "were, as most anglers are, quiet men and followers of peace." He undertakes to prove it from the fact that four of the Apostles actually were fishermen, and these four taught all the others to fish. Thus worked Izaak Walton till he was over fifty years old.

But, oddly enough, he made money, and soon was able to move to larger quarters on Fleet Street. Ironmongery was evidently all the thing in the days of the English Civil War. So when the great battles were over and there was peace, iron peace, under Oliver Cromwell, Izaak Walton gave up his London life, and bought himself the thing of which all anglers dream—a little place in the country, his own country—and all his dreams came true.

From then on, for some forty years, Izaak Walton spent a life of leisure, or of leisure broken with leisurely activity. At times he was on his own little place; at times he wandered about the country a welcome and indefinite guest, an old man who never grew older, who had said good-bye to the world and its troubles, and to whom Roundhead and Royalist were all one. Especially he sought, and was welcome in, the homes of the clergy. He had been greatly assisted in his London days by the famous Dr. John Donne, Vicar of St. Dunstan's. Both his wives, for he married twice, were of clerical families; he seems to have borne married life easily, a basis, as with some among us now, from which to go fishing. For his last twenty years he wandered and fished alone. When he died he left his little place to the poor of the parish.

He wrote his *Compleat Angler,* so to speak, while angling. The first edition of it was mainly thought out in his Fleet

Street days, the fruit of odd holidays and chance journeys. But later, with copious leisure and larger experience, he kept finding new things to put into the book, new verses, new jests and even new people.

As even casual readers remember, *The Compleat Angler* is built up on talks between various characters. They meet and go fishing together and they talk; or they can't go fishing, so they talk; or they come in from fishing and they talk. Some of us do it still. And in among the talk they have so many pleasant cups of ale and draughts of the "best barley wine," that it's a pleasure to be with them; plenty to smoke, also, from the long pipes of the period, for tobacco, in spite of King James I, had now come into its own. Indeed, the comfortable entertainment begins in Chapter 1, page 1, paragraph 1, of *The Compleat Angler*. An angler, *Piscator*, accosts two travellers on the road with the words:

"You are well overtaken, Gentlemen! A good morning to you both! I have stretched my legs up Tottenham Hill to overtake you, hoping your business may occasion you toward Ware, whither I am going this fine fresh May morning."

"Sir," replies one of them, "I, for my part, shall almost answer your hopes; for my purpose is to drink my morning's draught at the Thatch'd House in Hoddesdon." . . .

So away they wander together, talking of fishing, so that the three miles to Hoddesden seem nothing, and there they are at the Thatch'd House, and must needs all enter together "for a cup of drink and a little rest."

What fisherman, then or now, could pass a Thatch'd House?

Thus it was with the freshness of the morning; but equally so with the pleasant weariness of the evening after a long day. "Come, Hostess, where are you? Is supper ready? Come, first give us drink and be as quick as you can for we are all very hungry. . . . Come, Hostess, more ale . . . and when we have supped, let's have your song!"

The early people in these wayside talks were a fisherman,

Piscator, and a traveller, *Viator.* But later on Izaak thought it a good idea to let the second man be a huntsman, *Venator,* and then he put in a third who was called *Auceps,* which we understand to mean a falconer, a man who hunts birds with birds. Time has dropped him clean out. Today we would have to make him an Airman. That is probably exactly what Izaak Walton would have done, for he kept on putting in new things and new people till death made a final edition.

You ask perhaps, I hope not with impatience, what we can learn from Izaak Walton. Why, don't you see we've learned a lot already; that fishing is the Apostles' own calling; that fishing must be carried on in an atmosphere of good will and forbearance; that the longest story must never seem prosy; that a cup of ale beneath a tree is better than a civic banquet, and an old familiar song from a familiar singer outclasses grand opera.

And you can also learn, or learn over again, the peculiar and manifold charm of our English language. For what Izaak Walton writes is sufficiently like our own speech to be familiar, and sufficiently unlike to have a quaintness of its own. He has a chapter, for example, which he entitles *How to fish for, and to dress, the Chavender, or Chub.* A witty English writer of today was so impressed by the conversion of the everyday chub into the romantic chavender that he followed it up with a gallop of analogous synonyms:

> There is a fine stuffed Chavender
> A Chavender, or Chub,
> That decks the rural pavender,
> The pavender, or pub,
> Wherein I eat my gravender,
> My gravender, or grub.

And so on, amazingly. But I must not further trespass on the good nature or the copyright of Mr. St. Leger whose complete poem may be found in the fascinating little anthology, *The Comic Muse.*

All these things you can learn from Izaak Walton. But if you ask what you can learn of the technique of fishing, the answer is that you can't learn anything at all. The apparatus of the modern expert, the knowledge of trout and flies, the mechanisms of reels—all these have left good old Izaak two centuries and a half in the rear. All that he can teach is the *spirit*; yet the performance in the long run rests on that.

To take an example, nowadays we always connect trout fishing with the art of casting flies—an exquisite art, indeed, when at its highest. What more beautiful than a cast far across a wide stream to where the broken water 'round the end of a sunken log marks where a trout must lie? What more beautiful indeed, except the ensuing leap of the foolish trout itself, a victim of its own delusion. It is an art that, personally, I can envy but not share; I can never catch anything that way except willow trees.

But at least I have the consolation that Izaak Walton is in my company. He knew very little about casting flies and that was not his ordinary method of catching fish anyway. He caught them, as I do, and perhaps you, with anything they would eat, taken off anything they would eat it on.

This seems odd in view of the long discussion in *The Compleat Angler* on fly fishing and how to do it and how to make flies. The discussion, moreover, has its setting in one of these charming sylvan scenes—under a sycamore tree with wine and a snack of food—which are the very inspiration of the book.

"It is now past five of the clock," says *Piscator*, meaning five in the morning; "we will fish till nine; and then go to breakfast. Go you to yon sycamore tree and hide your bottle of drink under the hollow root of it; for about that time, and in that place, we will make a brave breakfast with a piece of powdered beef and a radish or two that I have in my fish bag. We shall, I warrant you, make a good, honest, wholesome, hungry breakfast."

But, as a matter of fact, Izaak Walton did not himself write the discussion of the "making and using of flies" which follows. He knew that he ought to have something of the sort in his book so he got a fellow angler to write it in, thereby lifting his friend Mr. Thomas Barker to an immortal seat beside himself. Mr. Barker was by trade a cook and may have aided also in the hints on cooking fish ("dressing the chavender, etc.") that are freely inserted in the *Angler*. Mr. Barker is also said to have been a "humourist"; he may have helped with the jokes.

But all agree that when it comes to fishing with worms, grasshoppers and frogs, Izaak Walton was a past master. There is comfort here for those who suffer, as I do, from the insolent superiority of men who refuse to use bait. Izaak used nothing else. Indeed, many who knew very little about his book have heard the quotation from it about the use of a frog as bait: "Use him as though you loved him, that is, harm him as little as you may possibly, that he may live the longer." The implication of a slow death behind the apparently kindly words is one that might make the coldest-blooded frog boil with indignation.

But the point is that Izaak Walton was out to get the fish. In the same way, he and his friends were fond of using little floats tied to sticks or anchored in the stream. This with us is viewed among good sports as the last resort of ignoble minds. Indeed, the game laws forbid that kind of fishing to all except Indians on a reservation. But to Izaak and his friends it represented the very best of sport and the rarest of opportunity. They had only to choose a grassy sward beneath a spreading sycamore, among whose roots babbled the passing stream, to fix their floats, pour out a cup of ale, light a long pipe and open a discussion on the Gospel of St. John or listen to Mr. Barker tell in his own humorous way how to cook a carp—and there you were. Leave the rest to the frog.

Indeed, Izaak Walton is willing to go a little further with "bait" than the stomachs of more degenerate anglers could tolerate. He specializes on worms, distinguishing earth worms from drug-worms, worms found in excrement and in dead flesh such as the maggot or gentle worm; to which are added lob worms, brandling worms for which we search in cow dung, "horse dung being somewhat too hot and dry for that worm." Beside which an artificial fly on a bit of cardboard seems singularly clean and attractive.

Such dainty considerations are nothing to Izaak. He is out for fish. He'll go even further if we let him. "If you desire," he says, "to keep gentles, that is maggots, to fish with all the year, then get a dead cat and let it be fly-blown; and when the gentles begin to be alive and to stir, then bury it and them in soft, moist earth but as free from frost as you can; and these you may dig up at any time you intend to use them."

And there you are. But if you don't care to prepare the bait in this fashion, then Izaak explains to us a method of preparing the water of any likely pond, so as to make it attractive. "You are to throw into it," he directs, "either grains, or blood mixed with cow dung or with bran; or any garbage as chicken guts or the like."

If you are going to be an angler, the thing is to be a complete one. . . .

One might think that at least the discussions on cooking would be helpful, especially to us now in wartime days when we want to make the most of all kinds of food, and turn even coarse fish into something edible. The carp itself, the very fish which *The Compleat Angler* helps us to turn into a dainty dish, is very commonly thrown away with us in Canada as worthless—or else, if I may say it without offence, exported to the United States. Izaak Walton, I say, shows how to turn it into a dainty dish, and no doubt succeeded in doing it. But his process is quite beyond us. Here is the recipe:

"Put the Carp in a kettle; take sweet marjoram, thyme and parsley, each a handful; a sprig of rosemary and another of savoury; put them into two or three small bundles, and put them to your Carp with four or five whole onions, twenty pickled oysters and three anchovies—"

So far that's only about three dollars' worth of stuff, and you could gather it up in about a week, but wait:

"—Pour on your Carp enough claret as will cover him (lucky Carp!) and season your Carp well with salt, cloves and mace, and the rinds of oranges and lemons—"

We're up now to about ten dollars:

"—That done, cover your pot and set it on a quick fire till it be sufficiently boiled. Then take out the Carp; and lay it, with the broth into the dish, and pour upon it a quarter of a pound of the best fresh butter, melted and beaten with half a dozen spoonfuls of the broth, the yokes of two or three eggs and some of the herbs shred; garnish your dish with lemons and so serve it up. And much good do you!"

I think so, too.

Thus lived and wandered Izaak Walton from middle age to old age and then on to immortality. Especially was he welcome, we are told, "in the families of the eminent clergy of England of whom he was much beloved." Their kindness was returned. It was Izaak Walton's secondary interest, in the pauses of his leisure, to write biographies, or perhaps eulogies, of his departed friends and benefactors, lay or cleric. Here belong Sir Henry Wotton, Dr. John Donne, Bishop Sanderson and others. Their names, once known, now half-forgotten, still float down the stream of time with *The Compleat Angler*.

A Lecture on Walking

WALKING—it has come to that. They've taken away our motor cars, crowded us off the trains, cut out week-end excursions and drained the gasoline out of the motor boats. There is nothing for it, in the way of outdoor sport, but walking.

So let us make a virtue of necessity and all go in for walking.

On this understanding I would like to deliver a lecture, in set form like a college lecture, on the subject of Walking. It will be a great pleasure to me to do so, for it is now six years since an ungrateful college foiled me, on the mere ground of senile decline, to give any more lectures, and took away all my students. So now for a brief hour I want them all back, lined up on the benches to listen to a lecture on Walking. I want especially, not the younger ones, but those well into middle life, or even wheezing their way into old age; pleasant, puffy, comfortable-looking fellows as seen sitting in a leather armchair in a club but in poor shape if you start them walking.

There! Line them up. You, sir, the large student on the left, you are, am I not right, the president of a bank? Well, you needn't put on any plutocratic airs in this class. I doubt if you could walk half a mile. You say you played left wing on the football team? I don't doubt it. But I want you all to understand, gentlemen, that it's no use your talking about exercise you took thirty years ago. That won't help you now. You, sir, just sitting down on my left, are, I believe, an Anglican Bishop. Now, don't tell me about your championship high jump in 1910. Everybody knows, on the side, that you jumped your way into your bishopric. How high could you jump now?

Now, gentlemen, please open your notebooks and write the heading WALKING, and then when I come to each important point, I'll tell you what to write. Don't write till I tell you. Remember how we used to do it.

You might begin, please, with a little note, *"Professor's own experience: a devotee of walking for many years: has walked the Montreal mountain every morning nearly as far as the cemetery."* On second thought, gentlemen, please delete the phrase, *"nearly as far as the cemetery."* It might be misunderstood.

And what is more, gentlemen, I am led by such walks to observe how little of walking for walking's sake survives today. It is my experience again and again to walk Mount Royal at nine o'clock in the morning and see not a soul in sight. The motor car, gentlemen, has grave sins to answer for in cutting us out from the air and exercise that once were ours. Look at yourselves, gentlemen: I need hardly say more.

Now will you please write in your notes, *"Definition of Walking,"* and for that I will ask you to turn to the *Encyclopaedia Britannica*, Volume 23, page 301, division 1, or, if you prefer it, don't turn to it but take my word for it, and write it at my dictation. "Walking is the art of progression by setting one foot methodically before the other and is the most venerable and universal way of locomotion among mankind, and has been for a million years." The same authority explains further, in regard to the technique of walking, that in plain straightforward walking one must not lift one foot into the air before the other has come down to the ground; in other words, the walker must not have both his feet in the air. This caution, in your case, gentlemen, makes me smile: I don't think there is much fear of any of you leaving the ground with both feet at once. All you need to understand from this is to distinguish *walking* in the proper sense from *shuffling*, which is what you do from your club lounge to your club dining room, and *shambling*, which is what you do when compelled to go along the street a hundred yards to look for a taxi.

Nor are we concerned here with the technique of walking when it becomes part of competitive athletics, for it's far too strenuous, I fear, for any of you. Walking in that form is, happily, dying out. Walking matches used to be held on a terrific scale two generations ago, both in England and in this country. Seven-mile walking races for an American championship were introduced in 1876, and in the present century the revival of the Olympic Games led to walking *marathons* on a scale of one to twenty-five miles. Walking, in this strenuous and distressing sense, seems to me, gentlemen, as no doubt to you, a ghastly business. I am thinking of walking only as the gentle and kindly exercise of the man who cannot spend his whole day indoors and must perforce be out in the open—as the relaxation of the office worker, tired of ink and paper and four walls, as the inspiration of the poet, and as the quiet *saunter* of the daydreamer.

I will ask you, gentlemen, to make a note here on that word *saunter*, as well illustrating our subject. Kindly mark it, "*Interesting note by professor on word* SAUNTER." This term, you will be surprised and delighted to hear, is one of the most curious in our language. It is derived from *Sainte Terre* (Holy Land). In early, pious days a knight with sins that needed absolution and a soul that needed redemption made a *Sainte Terre*, a Holy Land pilgrimage. This was originally a journey beset with danger, nobly braved.

Presently, with beautiful travel up the Mediterranean among olive groves and enchanted islands, the pilgrimage turned into a *saunter*, a delightful dream journey. So will you, too, find it, gentlemen, if you will take the practice of a daily walk. At first, you will find it a hard matter to gird up your loins (as near as you can find them) and step out three, four, five miles or more at a stretch. But with habit and continuance, and above all with the regularity that never misses, walking will become of such unconscious ease that you will, as it were, step out of yourself and find yourself *sauntering*—timeless, effortless, with no other thought beyond the quiet pleasure of not thinking. I cannot forbear to quote again from this high authority cited ahead, which thus expounds this aspect of a customary walk. "Walking in the nobler sense is a measured progress inspired of the woods and hills, by rivers and the flowers of the field, a serene partaking of the enduring sources of joy."

Well, gentlemen, with such an admirable ideal before us, I think we may now come down to particulars such as the question of companionship in walking, of hours and times and places, and the particular routine and regularity, if any, with which we see fit to surround it.

I begin, then, with the question of companionship. Should one walk alone, or is it better to walk with a companion? I think I hear a member of the class saying behind his hand, "What about women?"—and I may say I don't like the expression of his eye as he said it, nor the nudge he gave the student next to him, in whom I think I recognize one of our leading stockbrokers. Well, gentlemen, since the question of women has come up, I'll answer it. You are all, I am sure, elderly or, at any rate, discreet men, who would not, I am sure, repeat outside of the class anything said here in confidence. And in that sense I say, "Have nothing to do with going for walks with a woman." You will find her, gentlemen, a bore and a nuisance, or else you will find her too interesting, and in that case, gentlemen, there is no telling where your walks will lead you. Understand, gentlemen, that in this matter there can be no middle path. I am aware that some of you perhaps will say that you are able to associate with women as "comrades"—yes, that is the word—that you look on them as *comrades*. All I can say is that if you do, you are a nut. I had not intended to bring up this topic of walking with women, and will let it go at that. I will admit, of course, that you may, if you wish, go for a walk with your little granddaughter or grandniece of thirteen, provided that you make her keep her mouth shut. It will make a very pretty picture, your walking with her among the falling autumn leaves, especially if you keep well in the front of the picture yourself, and keep the child in the background.

But, far better, walk with a man of your own kind and size, and congenial in the sense that you have nothing in particular to say to one another. Silence, if deliberate, is artificial and irritating; but silence that is unconscious gives human companionship without human boredom. But if, by habit, you and your companion must talk, then take care to agree about everything all the time. Whatever he says, you say, "That's very true," and then you don't need to listen to what he's saying. If you miss a piece of it, you say, "That's very true when you come to think of it," and by that means you don't need to come to think of it at all. . . . There is, indeed, no better companionship than this trudging along, almost without conversation, but not quite, or at best with a repetition of the same remarks that have done duty between you already for years past.

Above all, gentlemen, avoid walking with a nature lover. Nothing spoils a walk so much as the observance of "nature"; I mean the details of the coming and going of birds, of the arrival of the first woodpecker and the departure of the last crow, and the first touch of green on the willow and the last seared yellow of the birch leaf. Leave all that stuff out. When you're walking, you're just out-of-doors—that's all. You're not an almanac.

A gentleman in the class asked me, "How long should one walk every day, to call it walking?" The question is an excellent one, so excellent that I was coming to it anyway. I will answer thus, "The ideal walk should last up to the point where one is *comfortably tired*. That happy phrase covers it all. Some of you, I fear, would be uncomfortably tired in about a quarter of an hour. But a man in any sort of condition has not begun to walk till he has walked for half an hour. Observe that a man's duties in the daytime generally prevent him from taking a real walk in the earlier hours of the day. Hence, to practise walking, probably the walker must walk twice a day. The morning walk of a mere half-hour before office or lecture time is rounded out by the real walk when the day's work is done and dinner still two hours away. You must come in, gentlemen, from your walk to your food; that is the real sequence: half an hour before breakfast or half an hour before lunch, and then the real thing, a six-mile walk (two hours), and come in *comfortably tired* to dinner with such an appetite as you have never had since you left the old farm, which all successful men in this country left at the age of twelve.

You will perhaps object that after such a walk you would be good for nothing in the evening. Quite so. That's what you ought to be good for. But, my dear sir, if you will let me say it to you quite frankly, what good do you think you are in the evening anyway? What you mean is that if you don't walk and don't take any exercise in the open air in the afternoon, then after dinner you can get half "lit up," and "go strong"—I think that was your phrase—till one in the morning. That's right, and go all flabby when you get up the next morning.

But how much better to get that comfortably tired feeling, to eat that marvellous dinner, and after it to sit down in front of a good fire, with a pipe of tobacco and a book of Ancient History, and a decanter in sight out of the corner of your eye—and then, in less than no time, off you drowse to sleep—the book, the decanter, the pipe, all forgotten—and stay asleep till bedtime. . . .

That's what walking will do: and that is why it has lasted a million years.

But, gentlemen, I hear your motor cars outside. Your chauffeurs are getting impatient. The class is dismissed.

Good-bye, Motor Car!

FOR the time being, the pleasure use of the motor car has disappeared from our world. It is likely that it will be a long time in coming back. Even the earliest victory that we can reasonably expect must be followed by a strenuous period of reproduction and restoration during which the world's depleted rubber supply will be absorbed in more essential operations than those of motoring for pleasure.

It is only now that we realize to what extent the motor car had come to shape and fashion all our leisure. Older and slower things were pushed aside, compressed into small compass or speeded up into newer and bigger forms. Golf changed from a quiet pursuit in a local pasture beside the town to a vast, mechanized organization carried on twenty miles from everywhere and transforming farms and fields to a clipped landscape of little flags, and a palace club house that grew and grew till it's become too expensive for its own members. People used to play golf in the ex-cow-pasture at five dollars a year. Lately they were just able to keep up their annual fee by never going out to play. It was the motor car that did this.

During the same period the motor car killed fishing. Sitting in a punt at one end of a rod was too slow; fishing around home at the old rate of two bites an hour, two bass a day, and two drinks a man, was just hopeless as beside a motor trip one hundred miles to Lake Katchehoochee, where you can get a motor boat for only ten dollars, and a man to run it for five dollars, and where there's the fine big Katchehoochee Inn, all built of spruce logs set on end, with piazzas and chromium cocktail bars and everything *à la carte* so as to cost more.

It was the motor car that did all that.

With fishing went boat sailing—the real old boat sailing in the real old sailboats. As far as I know, it has vanished from our inland waters. It survives only beside the open sea where people must use real sailboats and do real sailing in them or get drowned.

But on the inland waters there is no time for that. Sailing has given place to a sort of aquatic circus in a thing called a sailing dinghy, all bottom and no sides, all gunwale and no seats, all sail and no place to pour a drink. It has to be that way, because sailing has to be done in a form to fit in with driving a motor car ten to twenty miles to a sort of sailing meet, where a whole flight of dinghies skim over the water, as beautiful to look at as all such wicked things are.

Boys and girls in bathing suits line the gunwales of the boats—in bathing suits because, of course, they expect to be upset. They feel disgraced if they don't get upset; in the old days we felt disgraced if we did. There they sit, like birds on a swaying bough, wonderfully dexterous, tanned and bronzed and coloured and trimmed till they look as good as an advertisement. What they do is wonderful, but it isn't worth doing, or only for people who live so fast that they have no time for better.

But, above all, please do not let them think that that sort of thing is boat sailing, and that the contraption they are sailing in is a boat. A boat, a sailboat, used to mean, and still does mean beside the sea, a boat that is not meant to capsize, that is not meant to roll over sixty degrees in every squall. You don't "hang on" to a real sailboat because you are inside it—smoking. You don't have a row of girls sitting out on the gunwale because in a real sailboat you don't use girls. You may "take them out" on a fine afternoon with a wind that is guaranteed neither to rise nor to fall, but real sailing, as it used to be, was too long and too slow to be enjoyed by a mixed community of souls. . . .

Nowadays, you see, the whole of the dinghy sailing is

planned on the idea that, of course, you will all be back in time to dance at the Club House, or the Chop House, or the Old Windmill, or wherever the crowd will fly to after the sailboats are all capsized. . . .

But the old boat sailing was planned as a thing in itself, to take all afternoon if one only had an afternoon, all day if one had a whole day, all the end of the week from Friday till Monday (oddly enough we never called it the "week end"—that was a fashionable English term that sounded affected) . . . but, as I say, from Friday to Monday if you had all that, and then, for a vacation, sailing joined hands with camping, and there you were.

The scenes where the sailing and camping were done were the inland lakes like Lake Simcoe and Lake Couchiching which lie beside me, one to the right and one to the left, as I write this article . . . beautiful lakes, two among hundreds. Before the motor car came, their waters were flecked with the sails of real sailboats—large sloops half-decked, heavily ballasted, with a main boom that would kill an ox if you let it jibe; Mackinaw two-masted boats patterned from the Upper Lakes' fishing trade, bow and stern both sharp, the sternpost six to seven feet high, a cuddy forward and the rest open; and, with these, the boats we then called "yachts"— deep-draft boats with leaded keels, decked over, with a cabin with a folding table and four bunks . . . and with these again a great number of smaller sailboats, every one seaworthy.

A dinghy of today in a fair breeze would pass all this old fleet as if it weren't there. But then the old fleet would just sail on anyway, still smoking and with the sheets tied, against the rule that everybody made and everybody broke.

You see, they wouldn't care about the empty dinghy swishing by them because they are "going camping," and are down to the hatches with cargo. This, you see, is not a sail at all, but a voyage.

You notice the mattresses all rolled up tight and stowed under the foredeck, so that they will only get half-wet instead of completely soaked . . . there are the dunnage bags in which each man has his other duck trousers; there's the box full of canned food and the other one with the jar of whiskey and the keg of lager . . . lying on top of this stuff— for after all you need something to read—is a copy of a paper called *Tit-bits*. It will last three men four days because it is all made up of little bits about the height of the Pyramids, and you can begin anywhere and stop any time. That is how Lord Northcliffe made a fortune.

So away blows the old sailboat farther and farther out on the lake till all you see over the waves is just the bobbing patch of white that is the mainsail.

Perhaps, some day, it may turn around and come back again.

But meantime the motor car killed out the sailboat and with it the camping that was its associate. Camping was too slow. Why go and cut down spruce saplings for tent poles, and make a fire with smoke in your eyes, and sleep beside snakes when you can take your car and hire a cabin for a dollar a night for one, and only three dollars a night for two, and have supper at the Spruce Bough Inn with dancing. . . .

The motor car did that. It did it all. The only amusement for a youth came to be going out in a car with a girl, or going out in a car to look for a girl, or going out with a girl to look for a car. Since you can't drive all the time, they had to invent the pop and hot dog stand, and since you can't stand and eat all evening, they had to build a dance hall beside the pop stand.

You can't dance forever, so that had to expand into a sort of Inn, called the Old Saw Mill, or the Old Forge, or the old anything at all that a new thing isn't.

With that, money, money, money every minute . . . money for gasoline, money for pop, money for ice cream, more money for more gas, money for the right to dance, money for the right not to dance . . .

Thus staggered the world along, bankrupt with its own pleasure . . . the rich bankrupted by the richness of their golf club . . . the young bankrupted on soft drinks; the old bankrupted on hard ones. There was a time—it's not so long ago but what some of us can remember it still—when a young man could have a wonderful summer holiday on twenty-five dollars a month . . . along with one or two other young men with the same ideas and the same funds. You needed a sailboat and a canoe in tow, an extra shirt each and that extra pair of duck pants I spoke of. . . .

Things like bread and milk and butter and eggs cost nothing . . . you just went to the nearest farmhouse with an empty basket and ten cents—the farmer wouldn't take the ten cents; one ten-cent piece lasted all summer. As to drink, it cost hardly anything . . . no young people drank much before prohibition . . . out camping, if we came to a town, there was a bar with drinks at five cents. Two of those lasted three days. . . . There were no girls in it, but when you came home, all tanned up from a trip like that, you could get engaged to just about any girl you wanted.

So that's that. The pleasure car is gone. We won't pretend that we don't want it back. But there is no such thing as an unalloyed blessing or an unmitigated cure . . . let us look around for that old canoe; is it still somewhere in the back of the shed? Or is it lying somewhere on a bend of the river under the trees? And the heavy old sailboat with the bluff bow . . . is that it I see thumping, thumping toward us? . . . *"Ahoy-y-y!"* Let's get our things ready; hurry up; it's beating toward us. It will be right in at the dock in two hours.

So, good-bye, motor car. . . .

II

STEPHEN LEACOCK COULD TAKE A HEAVY, PONDEROUS SUBJECT, SHAKE ALL THE WEIGHT OUT OF IT, AND PRESENT IT IN A LIGHT, INTERESTING VEIN. HE HAS DONE THIS IN "COMMON SENSE AND THE UNIVERSE," "AN APOLOGY FOR THE BRITISH EMPIRE," AND "BRITAIN AND CANADA: OLD PHASES AND NEW." OF THE LAST TWO IT MIGHT FURTHER BE SAID THAT FOR OVER THIRTY YEARS STEPHEN LEACOCK TAUGHT HIS HONOUR STUDENTS IN ECONOMICS, OF CANADA AND THE EMPIRE. IN A SKETCH WRITTEN AT HIS DEATH BY PROFESSOR JOHN T. CULLITON, ONE OF HIS YOUNGER COL-LEAGUES, MR. CULLITON REMARKS: "HIS LECTURES WERE CROWDED. ADAM SMITH, JOHN STUART MILL, AND MALTHUS WOULD COME TO LIFE. HE, BEFORE WINSTON CHURCHILL, SAVED THE BRITISH EMPIRE EVERY MONDAY, WEDNESDAY, AND FRIDAY, AT THREE O'CLOCK, IN ROOM 20."

Common Sense and the Universe

I

SPEAKING last December at the annual convention of the American Association for the Advancement of Science, and speaking, as it were, in the name of the great 100-inch telescope under his control, Professor Edwin Hubble, of the Mount Wilson Observatory, California, made the glad announcement that the universe is not expanding. This was good news indeed, if not to the general public who had no reason to suspect that it was expanding, at least to those of us who humbly attempt to "follow science." For some twenty-five years past, indeed ever since the promulgation of this terrific idea in a paper published by Professor W. de Sitter in 1917, we had lived as best we could in an expanding universe, one in which everything, at terrific speed, kept getting farther away from everything else. It suggested to us the disappointed lover in the romance who leaped on his horse and rode madly off in all directions. The idea was majestic in its sheer size, but it somehow gave an uncomfortable sensation.

Yet we had to believe it. Thus, for example, we had it on the authority of Dr. Spencer Jones, the British Astronomer Royal, in his new and fascinating book of 1940, *Life on Other Worlds*, that "a distant universe in the constellation of Boötes has been found to be receding with a velocity of 24,300 miles a second. We can infer that this nebula is at a distance of 230,000,000 light-years." I may perhaps remind my fellow followers of science that a light-year means the distance travelled in one year by light, moving at 186,000 miles a second. In other words, this "distant universe" is now 1,049,970,980,000,000,000,000 miles away!

"Some distance!" as Mr. Churchill would say.

But now it appears that that distant universe has *not* been receding at all; in fact, it isn't way out there. Heaven knows where it is. Bring it back. Yet not only did the astronomers assert the expansion, but they proved it from the behaviour of the red band in the spectrum, which blushed a deeper red at the revelation of it, like the conscious water that "saw its God and blushed" at Cana in Galilee long ago. One of the most distinguished and intelligible of our astronomers, Sir Arthur Eddington, had written a book about it, *The Expanding Universe*, to bring it down to our level. Astronomers at large accepted this universal explosion in all directions as calmly as they once accepted the universal fall of gravitation, or the universal death in the cold under Carnot's Second Law of Thermodynamics.

But the relief brought by Professor Hubble is tempered, on reflection, by certain doubts and afterthoughts. It is not that I venture any disbelief or disrespect toward science, for that is as atrocious in our day as disbelief in the Trinity was in the days of Isaac Newton. But we begin to doubt whether science can quite keep on believing in and respecting itself. If we expand today and contract tomorrow; if we undergo all the doubled-up agonies of the curvature of space, only to have the kink called off, as it has been; if we get reconciled to dying a martyr's death at one general, distributed temperature of 459 degrees below zero, the same for all, only to find that the world is perhaps unexpectedly warming up again—then we ask, where are we? To which, of course, Einstein answers, "Nowhere," since there is no place to be. So we must pick up our little book again, follow science, and wait for the next astronomical convention.

Let us take this case of the famous Second Law of Thermodynamics, that inexorable scroll of fate which condemned the universe—or at least all life in it—to die of cold. I look back now with regret to the needless tears I have wasted over that, the generous sympathy for the last little band of survivors, dying at 459 degrees below our zero ($-273°$ centigrade), the absolute zero of cold when the molecules cease to move and heat ends. No stove will light at that, for the wood is as cold as the stove, and the match is as cold as both, and the dead fingers motionless.

I remember meeting this inexorable law for the first time in reading, as a little boy, a piece of "popular science" entitled *Our Great Timepiece Running Down*. It was by Richard Proctor, whose science-bogeys were as terrifying as Mrs. Crow's *Night Thoughts*, only slower in action. The sun, it appeared, was cooling; soon it would be all over. Lord Kelvin presently ratified this. Being Scotch, he didn't mind damnation and he gave the sun and the whole solar system only ninety million years more to live.

This famous law was first clearly enunciated in 1824 by the great French physicist, Nicolas Carnot. It showed that all bodies in the universe kept exchanging their temperature— hot things heated cold, and cold things chilled hot. Thus they pooled their temperature. Like the division of a rich estate among a flock of poor relations, it meant poverty for all. We must all share ultimately the cold of absolute space.

It is true that a gleam of hope came when Ernest Rutherford and others, working on radioactivity, discovered that there might be a contrary process of "stoking up." Atoms exploding into radioactivity would keep the home fires burning in the sun for a long time. This glad news meant that the sun was both much older and much younger than Lord Kelvin had ever thought it was. But even at that it was only a respite. The best they could offer was 1,500,000,000 years. After that we freeze.

And now what do you think! Here comes the new physics of the Quantum Theory and shatters the Second Law of Thermodynamics into gas—a word that is Dutch for chaos. The world may go on forever. All of this because of the final promulgation of the Law of the *Quantum*—or, shall we say, the Law of Just So Much—of which we shall presently speak. These physical people do not handle their Latin with the neat touch of those of us who knew our declensions as they know their dimensions. Of course they mean *Tantum* —but let it go at that. *Quantum* is drugstore Latin, *quantum sufficit*. *Tantum* is the real thing—*Virgilium vidi tantum* ("I saw something of Virgil").

At this point I may perhaps pause to explain that the purpose of this article is not to make fun of science, nor to express disbelief in it, but only to suggest its limits. What I want to say is that when the scientist steps out from recording phenomena and offers a general statement of the nature of what is called "reality," the ultimate nature of space, of time, of the beginning of things, of life, of a universe, then he stands exactly where you and I do, and the three of us stand where Plato did—and long before him Rodin's primitive thinker.

Consider this. Professor Hubble, like Joshua, has called upon the universe to be still. All is quiet. The universe rests, motionless, in the night sky. The mad rush is over. Every star in every galaxy, every island universe, is at least right where it is. But the old difficulty remains: Does it go forever, this world in the sky, or does it stop? Such an alternative has posed itself as a problem for every one of us, somewhere about the age of twelve. We cannot imagine that the stars go on forever. It's unthinkable. But we equally cannot imagine that they come to a stop and that beyond them is nothing, and then more nothing. Unending nothing is as incomprehensible as unending something. This alternative I cannot fathom, nor can Professor Hubble, nor can any one ever hope to.

Let me turn back in order to make my point of view a little clearer. I propose to traverse again the path along which modern science has dragged those who have tried to follow it for about a century past. It was, at first, a path singularly easy to tread, provided that one could throw aside the inherited burden of superstition, false belief, and prejudice. For the direction seemed verified and assured all along by the corroboration of science by actual physical results. Who could doubt electricity after the telegraph? Or doubt the theory of light after photography? Or the theory of electricity after reading under electric light? At every turn, each new advance of science unveiled new power, new mechanism of life—and of death. To "doubt science" was to be like the farmer at the circus who doubted the giraffe. Science, of course, had somehow to tuck into the same bed as Theology, but it was the theologian who protested. Science just said, "Lie over."

Let us follow then this path.

II

When the mediaeval superstition was replaced by the new learning, mathematics, astronomy, and physics were the first sciences to get organized and definite. By the opening of the nineteenth century they were well set; the solar system was humming away so drowsily that Laplace was able to assure Napoleon that he didn't need God to watch over it. Gravitation worked like clockwork, and clockwork worked like gravitation. Chemistry, which, like electricity, was nothing but a set of experiments in Benjamin Franklin's time, turned into a science after Lavoisier had discovered that fire was not a thing but a process, something happening to things—an idea so far above the common thought that they guillotined him for it in 1794. Dalton followed and showed that all things could be broken up into a set of very, very small atoms, grouped into molecules all acting according to plan. With Faraday and Maxwell, electricity, which turned out to be the same as magnetism, or interchangeable with it, fell into its place in the new order of science.

By about 1880 it seemed as if the world of science was

fairly well explained. Metaphysics still talked in its sleep. Theology still preached sermons. It took issue with much of the new science, especially with geology and the new evolutionary science of life that went with the new physical world. But science paid little attention.

For the whole thing was so amazingly simple. There you had your space and time, two things too obvious to explain. Here you had your matter, made up of solid little atoms, infinitely small but really just like birdseed. All this was set going by and with the Law of Gravitation. Once started, the nebulous world condensed into suns, the suns threw off planets, the planets cooled, life resulted and presently became conscious, conscious life got higher up and higher up till you had apes, then Bishop Wilberforce, and then Professor Huxley.

A few little mysteries remained, such as the question of what space and matter and time and life and consciousness really were. But all this was conveniently called by Herbert Spencer the *Unknowable,* and then locked in a cupboard and left there.

Everything was thus reduced to a sort of Dead Certainty. Just one awkward skeleton remained in the cupboard. And that was the peculiar, mysterious aspect of electricity, which was not exactly a thing and yet was more than an idea. There was also, and electricity only helped to make it worse, the old puzzle about "action at a distance." How does gravitation pull all the way from here to the sun? And if there is *nothing* in space, how does light get across from the sun in eight minutes, and even all the way from Sirius in eight years?

Even the invention of "ether" as a sort of universal jelly that could have ripples shaken across it proved a little unconvincing.

Then, just at the turn of the century, the whole structure began to crumble.

The first note of warning that something was going wrong

came with the discovery of X-rays. Sir William Crookes, accidentally leaving around tubes of rarefied gas, stumbled on "radiant matter," or "matter in the fourth state," as accidentally as Columbus discovered America. The British Government knighted him at once (1897), but it was too late. The thing had started. Then came Guglielmo Marconi with the revelation of more waves, and universal at that. Light, the world had learned to accept, because we can see it, but this was fun in the dark.

There followed the researches of the radioactivity school and, above all, those of Ernest Rutherford which revolutionized the theory of matter. I knew Rutherford well as we were colleagues at McGill for seven years. I am quite sure that he had no original intention of upsetting the foundations of the universe. Yet that is what he did, and he was in due course very properly raised to the peerage for it.

When Rutherford was done with the atom, all the solidity was pretty well knocked out of it.

Till these researches began, people commonly thought of atoms as something like birdseed—little round, solid particles, ever so little, billions to an inch. They were small. But they were there. You could weigh them. You could apply to them all the laws of Isaac Newton about weight and velocity and mass and gravitation—in other words, the whole of first-year physics.

Let us try to show what Rutherford did to the atom. Imagine to yourself an Irishman whirling a shillelagh around his head with the rapidity and dexterity known only in Tipperary or Donegal. If you come anywhere near, you'll get hit with the shillelagh. Now make it go faster; faster still; get it going so fast that you can't tell which is Irishman and which is shillelagh. The whole combination has turned into a green blur. If you shoot a bullet at it, it will probably go through, as there is mostly nothing there. Yet if you go up against it, it won't hit you now, because the shillelagh is going so fast that you will seem to come against a solid surface. Now make the Irishman smaller and the shillelagh longer. In fact, you don't need the Irishman at all; just his force, his Irish determination, so to speak. Just keep that, the *disturbance*. And you don't need the shillelagh either, just the *field of force* that it sweeps. There! Now put in two Irishmen and two shillelaghs and reduce them in the same way to one solid body—at least it seems solid but you can shoot bullets through it anywhere now. What you have now is a hydrogen atom—one proton and one electron flying around as a *disturbance* in space. Put in more Irishmen and more shillelaghs—or, rather, more protons and electrons— and you get other kinds of atoms. Put in a whole lot—eleven protons, eleven electrons; that is a sodium atom. Bunch the atoms together into combinations called molecules, themselves flying round—and there you are! That's solid matter, and nothing in it at all except disturbance. You're standing on it right now: the molecules are beating against your feet. But there is nothing there, and nothing in your feet. This may help you to understand how "waves," ripples of disturbance—for instance, the disturbance you call radio—go right through all matter, indeed right through *you*, as if you weren't there. You see, you aren't.

The peculiar thing about this atomic theory was that whatever the atoms were, birdseed or disturbance, it made no difference in the way they acted. They followed all the laws of mechanics and motion, or they seemed to. There was no need to change any idea of space or time because of them. Matter was their forte, like wax figures with Artemus Ward.

One must not confuse Rutherford's work on atoms with Einstein's theories of space and time. Rutherford worked all his life without reference to Einstein. Even in his later days at the Cavendish Laboratory at Cambridge when he began, ungratefully, to smash up the atom that had made him, he needed nothing from Einstein. I once asked Rutherford—it was at the height of the popular interest in Einstein in 1923—what he thought of Einstein's relativity. "Oh, that stuff!" he said. "We never bother with that in our work!" His admirable biographer, Professor A. S. Eve, tells us that when the German physicist, Wien, told Rutherford that no Anglo-Saxon could understand relativity, Rutherford answered, "No, they have too much sense."

But it was Einstein who made the real trouble. He announced in 1905 that there was no such thing as absolute rest. After that there never was. But it was not till just after the Great War that the reading public caught on to Einstein and that little books on "Relativity" covered the bookstalls.

Einstein knocked out space and time, as Rutherford knocked out matter. The general viewpoint of relativity toward space is very simple. Einstein explains that there is no such place as *here*. "But," you answer, "I'm here; here is where I am right now." But you're moving, you're spinning around as the earth spins; and you and the earth are both spinning around the sun, and the sun is rushing through space toward a distant galaxy, and the galaxy itself is beating it away at 26,000 miles a second. Now, where is that spot that is here! How did you mark it? You remember the story of the two idiots who were out fishing, and one said, "We should have marked that place where we got all the fish," and the other said, "I did; I marked it on the boat." Well, that's it. That's *here*.

You can see it better still if you imagine the universe swept absolutely empty: nothing in it, not even *you*. Now put a *point* in it, just one point. Where is it? Why, obviously it's nowhere. If you say it's right there, where do you mean by there? In which direction is there? In *that* direction? Oh! Hold on, you're sticking yourself in to make a direction. It's in *no* direction; there aren't any directions. Now put in another point. Which is which? You can't tell. They *both* are. One is on the right, you say, and one on the left. You keep out of that space! There's no right and no left. Join the points with a line. Now you think you've got something, and I admit this is the nearest you have come to it. But is the line long or short? How long is it? Length soon vanishes into a purely relative term. One thing is longer than another: that's all.

There's no harm in all this, so far. To many people it's as obvious as it is harmless. But that's only the beginning. Leave space alone for a moment and take on time and then things begin to thicken. If there is no such place as here, a similar line of thought will show that there's no such time as now—not absolutely now. Empty the universe again as you did before, with not a speck in it, and now ask, What time is it? God bless me, how peculiar! It isn't any time. It can't be; there's nothing to tell the time by. You say you can feel it go; oh, but you're not there. There will be no *time* until you put something into space with dimensions to it—and then there'll be time, but only as connected somehow—no knowing how—with things in space. But just as there is no such thing as absolute top or bottom in space, so there is a similar difficulty as to time backward and time forward.

The relativity theory undertakes to explain both space and time by putting them together, since they are meaningless without one another, into a compound called "space-time continuum." Time thus becomes, they say, the fourth dimension of space. Until just recently it was claimed further that to fit these relationships together, to harmonize space and time, space must have a curve, or curvature. This was put over to the common mind by comparing what happens in space with what happens to a fly walking on a sphere (a globe). The fly walks and walks and never gets to the end. It's curved. The joke is on the fly. So was the joke long ago on the mediaeval people who thought the world was flat. "What happened to the theory of the earth," writes Eddington, "has happened also to the world of space and time."

The idea was made plainer for us by comparing space-time to an onion skin, or rather to an infinite number of onion skins. If you have enough, you can fill all space. The universe is your onion, as it was Shakespeare's oyster.

The discovery by Einstein of this curvature of space was greeted by the physicists with the burst of applause that greets a winning home run at baseball. That brilliant writer just mentioned, Sir Arthur Eddington, who can handle space and time with the imagery of a poet, and even infiltrate humour into gravitation—as when he says that a man in an elevator falling twenty stories has an ideal opportunity to study gravitation—is loud in his acclaim. Without this curve, it appears, things won't fit into their place. The fly on the globe, as long as he thinks it flat (like Mercator's map), finds things shifted, as by some unaccountable demon, to all sorts of wrong distances. Once he gets the idea of a sphere, everything comes straight. So with our space. The mystery of gravitation puzzles us, except those who have the luck to fall in an elevator, and even for them knowledge comes too late. They weren't falling at all: just curving. "Admit a curvature of the world," wrote Eddington in his Gifford Lectures of 1927, "and the mysterious agency disappears. Einstein has exorcised this demon."

But it appears now, fourteen years later, that Einstein doesn't care if space is curved or not. He can take it either way. A prominent physicist of today, head of the department in one of the greatest universities of the world, wrote me on this point: "Einstein had stronger hopes that a general theory which involved the assumption of a property of space, akin to what is ordinarily called curvature, would be more useful than he now believes to be the case." Plain talk for a professor. Most people just say Einstein has given up curved space. It's as if Sir Isaac Newton years after had said, with a yawn, "Oh, about that apple—perhaps it wasn't falling."

Now with the curve knocked out of it, the space-time continuum, with these so-called four dimensions, becomes really a very simple matter; in fact, only a very pretentious name for a very obvious fact. It just means that information about an occurrence is not complete unless we know both where it happened and when it happened. It is no use telling me that Diogenes is dead if I didn't know that he was alive.

Obviously "time-when" or "place-where" are bound together and coexist with one another. If there were no space—just emptiness—there could be no time. It wouldn't count itself. And if there were no time, there could be no space. Start it and it would flicker out again in no time—like an electric bulb on a wobble-plug. Space-time continuum is just a pretentious name for this consequence of consciousness. We can't get behind it. We begin life with it, as the chicken out of the egg begins with its cell memory. All the mathematics based on "space-time continuum" get no further, as far as concerns the search for reality. It gets no further than the child's arithmetic book that says, "If John walks two miles every day for ten days," etc., etc. The child hooks space and time with a continuum as easily as the chicken picks up gravel.

III

But, unhappily, we can't get away from the new physics quite as simply as that. Even if we beat them out on space and time, there is far worse to come. That's only the start of it, for now, as the fat boy in *Pickwick* said, "I'm going to make your flesh creep." The next thing to go is cause and effect. You may think that one thing causes another. It appears that it doesn't. And, of course, when cause and effect go, the bottom is out of the universe, since you can't tell, literally can't, what's going to happen next. This is the consequence of the famous Quantum Theory, first hinted at by Professor Max Planck about forty years ago and since then scrambled for by the physicists like dogs after a bone. It changes so fast that when Sir Arthur Eddington gave the Gifford Lectures referred to, he said to his students that it might not be the same when they met next autumn.

But we cannot understand the full impact of the Quantum

Theory in shattering the world we lived in, without turning back again to discuss time in a new relation, namely, the forward-and-backwardness of it, and to connect it up again with the Second Law of Thermodynamics—the law, it will be recalled, that condemns us to die of cold. Only we will now call it by its true name—which we had avoided before— as the Law of Entropy. All physicists sooner or later say, "Let us call it Entropy," just as a man says when you get to know him, "Call me Charlie."

So we make a new start.

I recall, as some other people still may, a thrilling melodrama called *The Silver King*. In this the hero, who thinks he has committed a murder (of course, he hasn't really), falls on his knees and cries, "Oh, God, turn back the universe and give me yesterday." The supposed reaction of the audience was, "Alas, you *can't* turn back the universe!"

But nowadays it would be very different. At the call, the Spirit of Time would appear—not Father Time, who is all wrong, being made old—but a young, radiant spirit in a silver frock made the same back and front. "Look," says the Spirit, "I'm going to turn back the universe. You see this wheel turning around? Presto! It's going the other way. You see this elastic ball falling to the floor? Presto! It's bouncing back. You see out of the window that star moving west? Presto! It's going east. Hence accordingly," continues the Spirit, now speaking like a professor, so that the Silver King looks up in apprehension, "time, as evidenced by any primary motion, is entirely reversible so that we cannot distinguish between future time and past time: indeed, if they move in a circle both are one."

The Silver King leaps up, shouts, "Innocent! Innocent!" and dashes off, thus anticipating Act V and spoiling the whole play. The musing Spirit, musing of course backwards, says, "Poor fellow, I hadn't the heart to tell him that this only applies to primary motion and not to Entropy. And murder, of course, is a plain case of Entropy."

And now let us try to explain. Entropy means the introduction into things that happen of a random element, as opposed to things that happen and "unhappen," like a turning wheel, good either way, or a ball falling and bouncing as high as it falls, or the earth going around the sun. These primary motions are "reversible." As far as they are concerned, time could just as well go backwards as forward. But now introduce the element of random chance. You remember how Humpty Dumpty fell off the wall? All the king's horses and all the king's men couldn't put Humpty together again. Of course not. It was a straight case of Entropy. But now consider a pack of cards fresh from the maker. Are they all in suits, all in order again? They might so arrange themselves, but they won't. Entropy. Take this case. You show a motion picture of a wheel spinning. You run it backwards; it spins the other way. That's time, the time of primary motion, both ways alike. Now show a motion picture of a waiter with a tray of teacups. He drops them; they roll in a hundred fragments. Now run it backwards; you see all the little fragments leap up in the air, join neatly into cups, and rest on the tray. Don't think that the waiter smiles with relief. He doesn't: He can't smile backwards: He just relaxes from horror to calm.

Here then is Entropy, the smashing down of our world by random forces that don't reverse. The heat and cold of Carnot's Second Law are just one case of it. This is the only way by which we can distinguish which of two events came first. It's our only clue as to which way time is going. If procrastination is the thief of time, Entropy is the detective.

The Quantum Theory begins with the idea that the quantities of disturbance in the atom, of which we spoke, are done up, at least they act that way, in little fixed quantities (each a Quantum—no more, no less), as if sugar only existed by the pound. The smallness of the Quantum is beyond comprehension. A Quantum is also peculiar. A Quantum in an atom flies around in an orbit. This orbit may be a smaller ring or a bigger ring. But when the Quantum shifts from orbit to orbit, it does not pass or drift or move *from one to the other.* No, sir. First, it's here and then it's there. Believe it or not, it has just shifted. Its change of place is random, and *not because of anything.* Now the things that we think of as matter and movements and events (things happening) are all based, infinitely far down, on this random dance of Quantums. Hence, since you can't ever tell what a Quantum will do, you can't ever say what will happen next. Cause and effect are all gone.

But as usual in this bright, new world of the new physics, the statement is no sooner made than it is taken back again. There are such a lot of Quantums that we can feel sure that one at least will turn up in the right place—by chance, not by cause.

The only difficulty about the Quantum Theory has been that to make the atomic "orbits" operate properly, and to put the Quantum *into two places at once,* it is necessary to have "more dimensions" in space. If they are not in one, they are in another. You ask next door. What this means I have no idea.

Nor does it tell us any ultimate truth about the real nature of things to keep on making equations about them. Suppose I wish to take a holiday trip and am selecting a place to go. I ask, "How far is it? How long does it take to get there? What does it cost?" These things all come into it. If I like I can call them "dimensions." It does no harm. If I like I can add other dimensions—how hot it is, how much gold it has, and what sort of women. I can say, if I wish, that the women are therefore found out to be the seventh dimension of locality. But I doubt if I can find anything sillier to say than the physicists' talk of ten and twelve dimensions added to space.

Let it be realized, I say, that making equations and functions about a thing does not tell us anything about its real nature. Suppose that I sometimes wonder just what sort of man Chipman, my fellow club member, is. While I am wondering, another fellow member, a mathematician, comes in. "Wondering about Chipman, were you?" he says. "Well, I can tell you all about him as I have computed his dimensions. I have here the statistics of the number of times he comes (t), the number of steps he takes before he sits down (s), his orbit in moving round (o), aberrations as affected by other bodies (ab), velocity (v), specific gravity (sp), and his saturation (S)." He is therefore a function of these things, or shall we say quite simply:

$$F \int \frac{s.v.o.sp.S}{t.ab}$$

Now this would be mathematically useful. With it I can calculate the likelihood of my friend's being at the Club at any particular time, and whether available for billiards. In other words, I've got him in what is called a "frame" in space-time. But just as all this tells me nothing of ultimate reality, neither do the super-dimensions of the new physics.

People who know nothing about the subject, or just less than I do, will tell you that science and philosophy and theology have nowadays all come together. So they have, in a sense. But the statement, like those above, is just a "statistical" one. They have come together as three people may come together in a picture theater, or three people happen to take apartments in the same building, or, to apply the simile that really fits, as three people come together at a funeral. The funeral is that of Dead Certainty. The interment is over, and the three turn away together.

"Incomprehensible," murmurs Theology reverently.

"What was that word?" asks Science.

"Incomprehensible; I often use it in my litanies."

"Ah, yes," murmurs Science, with almost equal reverence, "incomprehensible!"

"The comprehensibility of comprehension," begins Philosophy, staring straight in front of him.

"Poor fellow," says Theology, "he's wandering again; better lead him home."

"I haven't the least idea where he lives," says Science.

"Just below me," says Theology. "We're both above you."

An Apology for the British Empire

It is related of George III that a learned divine once presented to the King his new volume, *An Apology for the Bible.* "I did not know," said the simple monarch, "that the Bible needed an apology." It was explained to him that the word *apology* was used in its Greek meaning of a defence. It is in this sense that I want to offer an apology for the British Empire, a humble apology, as coming from a person without rank or honour, neither a statesman nor a general, but just a subject of the King, and glad to be one. Such qualifications as I have to voice the apology rest upon an English childhood, a lifetime mostly spent in Canada but with much knowledge at firsthand of the other Dominions, as well as of the United States.

There has been of late some queer talk and odd misunderstanding about the British Empire. Mr. Churchill has found it necessary to explain that we are not liquidating the Empire after the war. Others, on the contrary, have suggested that the parts of the Empire unable to look after themselves should be put under "international control." This is a status, a straitjacket, entirely fitted for blood-crazy Germans and treacherous Japanese, but scarcely for the people living in peace in the open freedom of the Empire.

Nor do we want to be internationalized, any of us, in the Empire; I don't, and the Canadians don't, and Nigerian boys don't, nor the Cingalese, nor the Bahamians, nor the shepherds that watch their flocks on the windswept Falkland Islands—none of us. How would you like international control for the United States? Or even for Chicago?

Such a notion can only come from a very feeble under-

52

standing of what the Empire is and does.

The British Empire covers one quarter of the globe (13,-353,000 square miles) and includes about one quarter (525,-000,000) of its inhabitants. It's a pity it's not bigger. It is made up of a group of six Associated Commonwealths and about fifty more or less dependent areas.

Constitutionally, the Empire is supposed to be held together by the Statute of Westminster, a British Imperial Statute of 1931. But that's just a "suppose." In reality, it is just held together by a vast gentlemen's agreement, and in the case of Ireland it isn't even gentlemenly.

The Statute of Westminster, indeed, is just a myth, a sort of idealization of unity or reality otherwise created. We keep it just as the Nigerian savages keep a wooden God with big glass eyes in the half-dark of a grass bungalow. People shake when they go in. So do our lawyers. But in plain logic the Statute won't stand overhauling. It was passed by the British Parliament in 1931, after advice from an imperial Conference, and then sent on to the Dominions. So far it has never been accepted, not on its face value. Australia never ratified it; meant to and never has yet. There seemed something fishy about it, some trick in it. So in twelve years they haven't touched it. South Africa ratified it; yes, indeed, they ratified it but with a local statute that ripped it to pieces. Canada didn't formally ratify it, but accepted it, took it as read, till they found that if it went into force it would tie up Canada hand and foot with no supreme public authority left. We can only amend our Constitution by an Imperial statute; in other words, by calling the Westminster Statute off. Newfoundland, shivering and starving with the depression, accepted the Statute and then gave up Dominion Status (1935) and crawled back into its little old colonial cot where it had slept since 1583. Ireland, call it Eire if you know how, never even looked at the Statute of Westminster. They made a Constitutional Amendment Act of their own (1936). By this the British King is King of Ireland; but not King of Ireland in

Ireland, only outside of it. To find the solution, turn to the back of the book. That's the sole connection of Ireland with the Empire, except its language. Even as to that, they're working hard to restore the old Gaelic. If they're not careful, they'll learn to speak it and then they'll be sorry.

I forgot—one Dominion ratified the Statute, New Zealand. But any British person, knowing New Zealand, would take that for granted. Down there they ratify anything as soon as they see the British trademark. New Zealand is New *Britain*, about 150 per cent British. The size of the group of islands is 110,000 square miles, upside down in the Pacific instead of right side up in the Atlantic. The same people exactly, English and Scots, with enough Irish to make an Irish vote, a thing you have in any British country, like pepper in a soup. In a population of 1,600,000, we may leave out the 80,000 native Maoris—great fellows, all admit, a big asset in any trouble. A! Kia! Kia! Come on, boys! The climate is just the same as "at home," with plenty of rough snow for the Scots down south, rain for the Irish and for the English, meadow land beside willows, and cricket and the bells of the Church of England. . . .

So that's the way the major parts of the Empire, the Associated Commonwealth, hang together, associated under the same King. In reality, not quite even that, for they have to accept him separately. As a matter of fact, King George VI didn't begin to reign in England till he had been reigning for a day in South Africa, and in Ireland he didn't reign for another day after that.

The Crown is the imperial link. Legally there is no other except, oddly enough, that Canada keeps up the appeal from its own law courts to the final decision of the British Privy Council in London. We get better justice. It must be better because it costs ten times as much, as our lawyers assure us on their return from pleading.

Associated also under the British Crown are all kinds of areas—islands, colonies, naval and military stations, protectorates, all around the globe. It's hard to count them: some are half in the Empire and half out. But they number about sixty units of government. At first sight they seem to defy classification but when you look close they seem to represent a beautiful symmetry of structure according to how much, how little or how not at all, they govern themselves. Canada governs itself. So does Southern Rhodesia—almost. The Governor, the Ministerial Cabinet and everything look real, but, actually, certain ground is "reserved." Nearly as much as is reserved, but not quite, by the Bahamas (West Indies, Class F, Partly White)—Parliament, but the Cabinet not exactly a Cabinet. The vote is granted to all who have a very small property qualification. Most haven't.

And so you pass on down through the grades and degrees till you come to the great protectorate of the tropics, the places where white men cannot live.

Take Nigeria as an example. It is a vast tropical river country sunk in the hollow side of West Africa; a huge place, with low coasts all surf and foam, swamps, jungles, fever and the sleeping sickness, then dense equatorial forests, then wide plains of grass, on into the heart of Africa to die in the desert. Nigeria covers half a million square miles—more than the whole Atlantic seaboard of the United States. There is a native population of 25,000,000 people. The climate never varies; each day is awful. White people cannot *live* there; those who survive go home. This was the famous Bight of Bengal where "for one that comes out there were ten who went in."

And how many white people do you suppose "hold down" this vast protectorate of 25,000,000 people? About two or three hundred. There are, in all, 5,000 whites, but a large proportion of these are missionaries, nurses and teachers, holding down a job, not a country, along with the clerks and traders of the steamship companies and the Staff of Government House. The whole Nigerian national defence (pre-war) consisted of three guns (3½ inches each), four battalions of infantry, one mortar and a signal school class. But even at that the whole army is black anyway, except the officers. That's how Nigeria is "held down" by imperialism. In other words, the people of Nigeria could rise up and kill all the whites in one day. But why should they? So could the people of Omaha, Nebraska, rise up and kill all the commercial travellers. But I doubt if they would care to.

How was this vast, undisturbed rule brought about? It was like this. The British are terribly lazy about fighting. They like to get it over and done with and then get up a game of cricket. In the tropics, cricket is played on coconut matting. Well, Nigeria grows one-half the world's coconuts. So there you are! What with playing cricket and learning how to mix gin fizz and to tie on one-piece, two-leg cotton pants, the place was civilized in no time. Not quite, of course. The British took away all the brutalities of savagery—the hideous human sacrifices of Ashanti—and left only its pleasant aspects such as polygamy. Cannibalism went right out as soon as the American canned food came in.

The Government? Yes, there's a real Government House at Lagos, with all the forms that go with it, but mostly the Nigerians, those inland, govern themselves under their own chiefs, Emirs and such. All the revenue raised in taxes wouldn't keep Chicago going for six months. As to religion, it's entirely free, but Mohammedanism beats Christianity to a standstill. Yet the few Christian converts are full of zeal, expecting the Day of Judgement any time, and all set for it with music.

Some natives, it must be admitted, want a change. They have had enough education to look around and compare themselves with other countries. They want to be like Canada: you can hardly blame them. So they talk in a vague way of a great Gold Coast Nation under the British flag—by taking in all the other odd lots between the Congo and Senegal. It may come some day, or something like it, but meantime this is not a political scheme, just a forlorn African fancy, like the Golden Gates and the Year of Jubilee! Longfellow's dreaming slave came from the Gold Coast.

Now, can any sane person think of setting up a European International Committee to look after Nigeria? And if "International" means British, we've got it already. If it means American and British, that's all right if they promise not to introduce baseball—after all, we saw them first.

Nigeria is just one of ever so many such areas, great and small. It is the biggest of them, next to India, but the pattern is the same all the globe around.

India is, of course, the Empire's problem. By all means give it self-government. But how do you do it? You can't start self-government with a civil war. In the United States, there was a century between the Stamp Act and the Civil War. But imagine the situation if the North and the South had been all ready to start the Civil War as soon as Independence was granted. That's India. There is no such thing as the Indian nation. There are in India over two hundred nations, as distinguished by distinct languages. The great mass of the Moslem races cannot tolerate the Hindu races, nor the Hindus the Moslems. The Hindus think the Moslems rough and uncultivated, people of physical force and not of the spirit. The Moslems think the Hindus a set of flabby intellectuals, not men at all. It's the difference between football players and divinity students. We have it in all the colleges. The football teams would liquidate the divinity students, only they're not allowed to. That's India. While the British stay, liquidation can't start.

An American lawyer would say, "Federate India." You can't. It won't. Inside the Moslems, the Sikhs refuse any rule but British. No Pakistan for them. All through Hindu India are the cast-out people, the "untouchables," the 60,000,000 people that the rest won't eat with, from whose hands they will not even take water. Are they to be slaves? You can't take freedom to men who treat 60,000,000 others as dogs.

There is no union in India but the British Raj and the

English language and the imported British transport and industrialism. India is a misfit. It was old when England began, full when England was empty, and fallen asleep over dead books when England learned to read with Shakespeare and think with Newton.

Except to Great Britain, India has no meaning for the Empire, no cohesion nor even any commercial interest. To us in Canada, it is utterly alien. We would never dream of letting in Indians, touchables or untouchables. We forbid their immigration, not by law but by a lawyer's trick. In Australia, they forbid it flat out. South Africa let them in till they began to swamp Natal, then shut the door. In all good will, there can be no co-operation between India and the Dominions, except by and through and because of Britain. Cut that out and it's all gone.

What can be done about India? International Control by a committee? They have two hundred and twenty-two nations already. Anyway they'd only send Mr. Gandhi in a loincloth to lie down and die on the committee's doorstep—it's called Swa-raj, or Swa-slush, or something. There's no answer. We always pick Gandhi up and feed him.

There is nothing to be done but wait. If and when the people in India agree, all of them, or most of them, on what they want, and cut out that hideous untouchable stuff, then, I am sure, they can have Dominion Government tomorrow.

So India must, for the present, stay as it is. You can't have a free united state till you have first a free united people. At present the Indians in India won't let one another be that.

India must stay and the Empire must stay. You can't mark it out with rule and compass as we mark out on a flat ground of empty prairie an Oklahoma or an Alberta before it is there. Such places can begin with a ready-made constitution put up over them like a circus tent, but you can't do that with older places. The Empire is a long product of history. It began as a mixed result of national defence and plundering the Spanish Main. It was hard to tell a patriot from a pirate. Some were both. Then it shifted into adventure and commerce and refugee settlement. Puritans sang in the wilderness, till they were too busy with business and stopped singing. Empire wars with France and Spain came and went, accepted like rounds in a prize fight. Then came the Independence of America. We are just getting over it after one hundred and sixty years. That started Australia and New Zealand.

The first Great War of 1793-1815 brought in more colonies than they could use. They gave back some, like Argentina. Then followed the wonderful era of free trade, with all men brothers, which was too good to be true—there weren't enough brothers. Then the scramble to partition Africa and Asia and everything left over. That's when many people first learned the word "imperialism" and learned to hate it. But that is half a century ago, as long ago and as far away as Rudyard Kipling's Mandalay.

That's not the Empire today. We know better now. The Empire today means co-operation of hundreds of millions of people, not on equal terms, but on decent terms. What would have been a hundred discordant states, each a powerless prey for rapacity to destroy, has turned into the united buttresses that held alone for a while the falling walls of a broken world.

We prefer to keep all this going under a set of mediaeval forms and observances, offices and dignities, that sound as the very converse of popular liberty and equality. We pretend that the King is an absolute sovereign and to make him look like it we surround him with Beef-eaters, Lords of the Buck-hounds, Norroy Kings at Arms, a Poursuivant Unicorn, a Red Dragon and an Officer of the Black Rod. Those are all actual offices, but in reality these people are as harmless as a pack of cards, ranking somewhere below a full house. And with that we have Dukes and Earls who pay feudal homages, giving the King dead birds once a year, other offices all gone except the salary, and salaries all gone except the offices, and an official list of precedence—it is a fact—that distinguishes seventy-one classes of British subjects before it even lets in

Gentlemen. The point of it all is that it works. People like a bit of humbug. If a reader of this article heard that the King had appointed him Keeper of the Swans, he'd be all over town with it in a minute.

That's the way we run the Empire. Now send us along that International Committee, and we'll invite them to a cricket match, and let them see all Australia beat half England, have a gin fizz with the Archbishop of Canterbury, and go home.

Britain and Canada

Old Phases and New

MANY of us are wishing now that we had learned more while we were still at school about the British Empire and how it is made up and how it works. Our recollection of the old school geography doesn't help us much. We recall a picture of the solar system in full swing, with a huge earth sweeping around an insignificant sun, and after that the names of the counties of Ontario and the capes of North America. But indeed the whole vast system which we call the British Empire presents in its structure such a mass of oddities and inconsistencies that not even the lawyers can understand it. Is it one solid unit, or just a collection of units, "freely associating" while they care to, and off somewhere else when they are ready to? There is supposed to be at the centre of it a body called the Privy Council, or more properly the Judicial Committee of the Privy Council, to decide all cases that arise in regard to the laws and constitutions of the Empire. This is a very pleasant thing for the lawyers, as they have to take long trips at some one else's expense (lawyers never travel on their own) from various parts of the Empire to see what the Privy Council thinks of some contested case. As a matter of fact, the Privy Council, made of wise, experienced men, far too wise to think on their own account, merely whisper to the visiting lawyers, "What do they think about the matter over in your country?" and they say, "Well, that's what we think, too. . . ." As a matter of fact, some parts of the Empire, namely Eire (don't call it Ireland) and South Africa, no longer consent to appeal to the Privy Council—which is a pity as they lose a lot of good will and friendly intercourse.

But, in reality, the British Empire doesn't hang together by any set of hard and fast statutes, such as the Statute of Westminster (1931) that everybody talks about and nobody understands. This statute was passed by the British parliament and declares, practically in the same breath, that the Empire is permanent and that it can be dissolved at will. Nor need the Americans laugh at this, since it is practically what their Constitution said from 1789 till 1865 about the relation of the States to the Federal Government. It took a whole Civil War to find out what it did mean.

We've learned, with the help of this American experience, a better system of dealing with our imperial constitution. We don't ask what it *means;* we just take it as a sort of "gentlemen's agreement." There are certain things which it is "the thing" to do, and others that you simply "don't do" because it's not "the thing" to do them. It's like the game of cricket—which many of you have now seen as played in England. When we play it in my home town of Orillia, or yours of Sussex, New Brunswick, or Red Deer, Alberta, there're lots of fighting and disputes in it, almost as good as American baseball, with argument and tumult around the umpire, so that you can't see which one he is till they carry him off the field. But in England cricket is cricket; you mustn't dispute or argue. It's not "the thing." If you're fielding at square leg (ask the nearest Englishman where that is) and you get a paste with the ball in the pit of the stomach, you mustn't complain; you must just say, "Sorry, old man." That's addressed to the bowler. Ask the Englishman why you say you're sorry for his sake; it wasn't his stomach.

What I am really trying to say is that all government rests, not on codes and laws (those are for criminals), but on decency, kindly feeling and a proper idea of the merits and rights and the good sides of others. This is especially true of our British Empire. We couldn't live a day without it. You should carry the idea up to the verge of truth, and for the sake of good fellowship, even a little beyond. I've had the good luck to see a great many parts of the British Empire and I make it a rule to praise it all. If a man says he comes from Jamaica, I say, "Ah, now there's an island! . . . if you like . . ." So it is; it's an island. And if a man tells me he's from Western Australia, I say, "My! my! What country, especially up inland past Calgourlie! How fertile! I've seen a cabbage growing there in the open without support. . . ." And for Prince Albert, Saskatchewan, "Ah, now there's a climate for you! Never cold; that is, never *severely* cold; never far below zero—in summer. . . ."

Nor do I say this to try to be funny. I mean it in earnest. And when you've done with your fellow Britisher, use it on an American and tell him that Nevada is your idea of a summer resort.

But just now we're to talk only of Britain and Canada and to illustrate various imperial phases through them. You may notice at once the difficulty, as all throughout the Empire, of finding suitable names. Britain. Where's that? When I was young, there was no such place outside of a poetry book. We always used to say "England"—to mean in a general sense— well, whatever "Britain" means now. A poet of the Crimean War days could write, "One more gone for England's sake, where so many go," though perhaps the man fallen in the snow was a Scotchman; and a learned professor could write a whole book called *The Expansion of England*, as if Ireland and Scotland hadn't swelled up, too.

Presently the other parts of—well, of what they are all parts of—got touchy about it. They wouldn't be called "England" any more. The Channel Islands were especially bitter. They considered that they had conquered England under their own Duke in 1066 and that England was therefore an annex of the Channel Islands. Believe it or not, this fiction was actually kept up till 1914; the British parliament didn't legislate for the Islands and had no power there except through the King—but not as King—as ex-Duke of Normandy. This fairyland fell under the shadow of the Great War Income Tax.

But what name could be used? "Great Britain" leaves out Ireland. "British Isles" won't fit in ordinary sentences. The "United Kingdom" is a law term. So now we say "Britain"; when we get settled to it, we shall talk of taking a trip to "Britain," which in my youth would have sounded like going to "Caledonia" or running over to "Erin."

The name "Canada" used to be just as bad but is now pretty well straightened out. Nobody knows where it came from. When Jacques Cartier came up the St. Lawrence in 1535 on his way to McGill University (then called Hochelaga), he came to the great river that we call Saguenay—in fact, the Indians told him that up this and beyond it, farther west, was the Kingdom of Saguenay, full of gold and diamonds; they were right in a way. Savage legend always has a background. They meant the Hollinger mine, and God's Lake and Flin-Flon, the legend of gold and silver beyond the divide, which later turned out to be true. But they told Cartier, also, that if he went on up the river he would come to "Canada," and when he got to where Quebec is they said, "This is Canada and beyond it is Hochelaga" (corner of McGill College Avenue and Burnside). . . . What did the name mean? We don't know. Some said it was Algonquin *Kanata*—the narrows; some said it was Algonquin *Kanada*—a collection of wigwams. Later some one made a joke, "It's Spanish *Aca-Nada*"—meaning "nothing there." That joke got into the schoolbooks of my youth as dead earnest (the education department in Ontario was Scotch) and stayed there. So we don't know. The French called the country *New France*—a name that was, so to speak, spilt on the American coast (1524) by Verrazano (he never landed north of New Hampshire), and then picked up again by Champlain. It was the official name of the country till the Conquest, but by about the year 1700 people commonly used "Canada" and even put it in official correspondence.

After the cession of 1763, the British government adopted

the name "*Quebec*" for its new possession, the reason being that General Amherst and General Murray both declared that they couldn't find out just how much territory the French meant by Canada. So Quebec it was, on a small scale, till 1774, and then it was the huge Quebec of the Quebec Act of that year, which reached from the Gulf of St. Lawrence to the Mississippi, and took in Chicago, what there was of it to take—mudflats, reeds and an Indian Portage—and perhaps a Rotary Club.

The schoolbooks may have led you to think that France and England fought for the possession of Canada (1754-1763). They didn't. They weren't thinking of it. They were fighting, so to speak, for the United States, for the marvellous Ohio territory just being revealed in all its park-land fertility. After the war the English didn't want Canada particularly, to which fact we owe a great deal of the freedom of our present institutions and especially the privileges of church and speech and nationality extended to French Canada, which alone made possible our Confederation.

A lot of the silly nonsense talked about Canada as a land of desolation began right then and has kept up till today. Voltaire's sneer about "the snow" passed down in history, and people forgot the last, wistful phrase of the departing Governor Vaudreuil, "A vast and beautiful country. . . ."

But I was talking of the name. "Canada" never got on the map till England decided to keep it and use it, after the loyalists came in, to name Upper and Lower Canada (now Ontario and Quebec) in 1791, and after that, in 1841, when they united the two together as the Province of Canada. That lasted till 1867 when the name "Canada" was used to cover all British North America—yes, all, because Newfoundland was invited in. But even long after that, forty years after that, people in the Maritimes used the term "Canada" to mean a separate place; within my own recollection—and mind you, I'm not even eighty—I've heard Nova Scotia people say they had never been in "Canada." . . . That's changed now. So, too, with the North West. "Canada" meant another country from their own till after 1869. . . . And with British Columbia till 1871. . . . The name triumphs now; it reaches from the forty-ninth parallel to the North Pole, in a long sort of wedge like a slice of orange peel. We own more of the North Pole than any other nation, except the Russians.

Even these casual references to history show something about where we got our relationships with Britain. Pretty thin they were at first. We "owned" the Maritimes (the huge Nova Scotia that reached to what was called Massachusetts) as far back as 1713. But what there was of them was all French. Then as the shadow of a new war fell, things began to happen. The British government deliberately founded Halifax so as to have a real footing in Nova Scotia, founded it mostly with old soldiers, all pipe clay and mitered helmets (see Mr. Jefferys' picture of the Foundation), but so unhandy on the land they couldn't even grow cabbages. So for that the government of England sent out a set of distressed Germans and located them at Lunenburg in Nova Scotia. There were always "distressed Germans" in those days, ready to be sent out to America. I forget what they were distressed about; something pretty tough, I hope.

Every mother and every mother country has a favourite child. Now Halifax, all hearty British as compared with the West Indies, all black, and with the American plantations, fractious and bothersome, was the favourite child of the mother country. And so the law officers of the Crown decided (that is, somebody whispered it to them) that the settlers had an inherent British right to an elected assembly. They got it in 1758 and that became, and is, one of the great precedents of the British imperial system. . . .

The dark side of this picture, the reverse of this bright medal, was the forcible moving out, the expulsion of the Acadian French of Nova Scotia, some 6,000 of them, shipped away, some here, some there, with no compensation for their land or their stock. It makes bad reading. The British government tried to plead that the imminence of a new war made these people a danger, as they might fight on the side of France. One hopes they would have. But tears have fallen for nearly a century over the pages of Longfellow's *Evangeline* which chronicles their fate.

That much there was of British . . . and out in the West the wide sovereignty of the Hudson's Bay Company, under their Charter of 1670, covered all the watershed of Hudson Bay, and, by extension, all the Pacific coast, over two million square miles. . . . It was all called Rupert's Land then (after the wonderful Prince Rupert who founded the Company. The name lasted officially till 1869. It only survives now in the name of the Province of Rupert's Land. But the North West—the common name for it—was far more Scottish than English. The Company's vessels sailed from London around Scotland to the Bay. Most of their men on the ships and at the forts were Scots—islanders at that. The canoemen and servants were French, or French half-breed Métis. The language of the West was French and Indian Cree, with Scottish for the parlour. . . . The West was empty till 1870. The Roman poet Virgil said that to found the Roman Empire was *tanta molis*—Latin for "a hell of a business." But he'd never seen Canada.

Through this maze of history, where did our government come in? Where did we get those privileges, presently rights, that gradually removed us from the control of Great Britain? As usual with British people, much of it was accident, much of it was done by the Turkish system of doing nothing, and much of it, most of it, a result of that inherent "decency" toward other people and toward those who can't hit back, that is the characteristic of the free government that grew up under British and American democracy. This democracy has not been the result of theory but of instinct and temperament; the fact came first and the theory afterwards. It is always thus; professors of theory merely hold post-mortems.

With us in Canada the sequence of development in our

relations with Britain ran like this: The grant of freedom of religion to the Roman Catholic French in Canada (1763) gave it, of necessity, to all Roman Catholics. In England they didn't have it till the emancipation of 1829. When the Loyalists came in (1784 and on), they had to have representative assemblies by virtue of the Halifax precedent and by what they had left at home. Here began Upper Canada's first government under Governor Simcoe. We may admit that Simcoe made it as aristocratic as he could; his little parliament at Niagara was all feathers, forms, uniforms, salutes of guns and speeches from the throne—in fact, just like "home." From him and from his senior Lord Dorchester, we carried down a lot of those queer formalities of government that mean so little to the cynic, so much to the philosopher. But aristocracy wouldn't work in Upper and Lower Canada (1791-1841). It broke down under the Rebellion of 1837, after which the British government hanged the rebels and adopted their programme. That gave the united province of Canada (1841-67) responsible government with a cabinet of its own, so that it controlled everything except foreign policy, trade and navigation, etc.—all local things. Old-fashioned Tories, like the Duke of Wellington, were reported "thunderstruck" when they heard of giving a colony its own government. But old-fashioned Tories always are thunderstruck. That's how they live; indignation keeps them warm. Cabinet government for the Province of Canada gave it automatically to the Maritimes.

Cabinet government failed to work in the Province of Canada, because the parties simply couldn't get a majority that was a majority in each section (Canada East and West) and of each race, and also of the whole.

Hence the plan of a wide union of all British North America. Everybody had talked of this for years as an ideal. But ideals never come true till something else happens. It was the American Civil War, that and the naughty Fenians who grew out of it, that chased all the scattered British North American

Colonies into Confederation like chickens into a coup. Great Britain was the mother hen herding them in, with a peck here and a push there—a railway for Nova Scotia, a railway for B.C.—and free leave for them all to divide up the Hudson's Bay Company's land. . . . In they came, and they couldn't get out.

Confederation in 1867, however, was on a different footing from our present relations. The British soldiers were still here till 1871; the British Navy at Halifax and Esquimalt till 1903. All foreign policy was managed from Downing Street—no Canadian ambassadors or ministers—treaties all made for us, though a Canadian might be invited to "sit in" and see it done, as Sir John A. Macdonald at the Washington Treaty of 1871. We couldn't even hang our own criminals at first (not till 1878), as the fountain of mercy only flowed from Downing Street through the Governor-General. But now the Minister of Justice runs the fountain from his own tap of tears.

So it was with all of it. Bit by bit the special reservations, treaty powers, etc., all wore away. The Red River Rebellion of 1869 was put down (frightened away) by mingled imperial regulars and Canadian militia. The Rebellion of 1885 was put down with all-Canadian forces, with only an imperial general running up and down to show them how—or how not, I forget which. . . . A string of Imperial Conferences presently turned the chief colonies into Dominions, and by the Great War of 1914 they were practically as free as Great Britain itself.

But the real thing was that Canada outgrew the idea of its own inferiority to Britain that had vexed its earlier years. No doubt the mingling of population in the great immigration (1900-1913) helped a lot by welding into the structure of the Dominion the temper of American and Scandinavian people —some newcomers, we may admit, didn't help much and in some spots the thing was overdone but in the main it helped to make a greater Canadian self-reliance. Other things helped also, other aspects of culture. British scholarship and learning; Latin and Greek, the seniority and sneeriority of Oxford, the dead weight of the classical tradition, sat heavy on the chest of Canadian academic aspirations. Ask any of us who spent years and years of study to get a B.A. degree at Toronto or Queens in the early Nineties, only to find that a better B.A. (in the world's eyes) could be got at Oxford in less time on brandy and soda. They had other degrees, too, I admit. This burden sat until presently it got heaved off by the rise of the great practical science schools in Canada, McGill and others, with all the water power of a continent thundering in their ears, with mines and mountains for geologists to rifle . . . schools, beside which the practical science schools of England were nursery games. Soon after 1900, hundreds of British students came over to "get science" in Canada as humbly as Canadian students went to pick up crumbs of Greek under the Oxford table. . . .

But at this point, with a lot still to say about British and Canadian culture, I must close. As the professors say to their classes, "That will be all for today," expecting a deep sigh.

Generals I Have Trained

IT is a great pleasure to me in these days, when war has shown how necessary preliminary training is, to look back to the fact that I have myself trained a very great number of army officers now serving at home and overseas. In particular, I have trained no less than six Canadian generals. So much so that I may regard myself, in a sense, as a professional general-trainer.

I thought nothing of it at the time. Those who can remember as far back as a little over fifty years ago will recall how little we thought then of military things. This was because it was known that war was quite obsolete and bygone, and was a thing only to be applied to savages such as the Matabeles and Mashonas. These were called "tribesmen," and it was understood that every now and then they would "rise" and when they rose they would be mowed down again by Mr. Gatling's new gun. After which the British government would lend them money to rebuild their kraals and they would crawl back.

But apart from that, there wasn't any idea that war could come back to us a terrific reality. In fact, we lived in a world of which no one of a later generation can ever dream. I remember in my student days in Toronto how ridiculous we thought a little group of obsolete students, way behind the time, who kept up military drill, calling themselves, "Company K" of the Queen's Own Rifles. They used to "form fours" out in front of the Varsity Building, with only two or three to each four, while we others stood around and laughed at them. You see, they had been organized in 1861 to repel the American Civil War and apparently they didn't know it was over.

71

One of them was called Howard Ferguson (even then very bossy; he was an officer, of course), and one afterwards wrote Flanders Field, and several others now sleep there. But all that we couldn't know. We stood and laughed. So did the world.

But the time when I came to train generals personally was just after that. I had become a resident master—the senior resident master—at Upper Canada College. This school had been founded originally with the idea of training (turning out, they called it) Christian gentlemen. That was all right as an ideal. As a matter of fact, it was found that the school had to turn them out before they got trained into Christian gentlemen. Those are hard fellers to make. In fact, the "gentleman" part of it proved quite impossible. I do not know to this day just how you train a gentleman. I admit he's unmistakable when he's trained and anyway you can tell him by his old school tie. But it didn't seem to work at Upper Canada College. Year after year the Principal used to announce from the platform in the Prayer Hall that this was a school for Christian gentlemen and that its aim was to train boys for a Christian life. Everybody was glad when they gave up the ideal of training Christians and it was announced that the school would train boys for the Royal Military College at Kingston.

That was a much better aim. And it was good musketry, too; aim low and you hit something. So for years after that and all through my resident time (1891-1899), one of the successful features of the work at Upper Canada College was training boys for the R.M.C. That's where my generals came in; they passed from me to the R.M.C.; from there (in those days) to the Imperial Army; and from there all over the globe. But I was the start.

Hence I thought it might be of use to record my methods in training generals. Well, in the first place, I began with kindness. When a new general came into my hands, I used to go along to his room and sit on the bed and talk to him, mostly about his home. Not a word about discipline, about his having to take a bath once a week and that sort of stuff. Give him a chance. He might want to do it. But just at first, kindness.

I recall in this connection one particular general, one of the smallest and sturdiest generals I ever trained—in fact, he looked hard and tough and bullet-headed even at eleven years old, this little general. He told me he'd come down all the way from the Yukon, had taken nearly a year to make the trip; spoke of his Husky dog teams that he'd used for his sleds and about his portages after the "break-up." I forget if he mentioned other people coming with him; at any rate, knowing him then and later, I'm sure that he didn't need them. He seemed to think a lot of the North but very little of the school and the staff. He said he doubted whether any of the masters he'd seen in the school that day would make much of a showing in a canoe. And he said he had a friend, a Siwash Indian, who could have thrown the Principal over the fence.

I recall the similar case of a general, newly arrived from Hamilton, Ontario, his home at the time, though his address just now is North Africa and Italy. He wasn't feeling so good, just sitting on the edge of his bed and looking downhearted. So I asked him where he came from and said Hamilton was a great place, and the general said it was the greatest iron and steel centre in Ontario. As he said it, the tears broke into his eyes at the thought of it. . . . I saw it mentioned in the papers the other day that he is a man of iron determination. They got it wrong—iron and steel, rolled iron, ingots and steel bullets—in other words, from Hamilton. Yet I am sure that he still keeps the softer side that I first saw. If anyone whispered, "What about Burlington Bay in the moonlight of June?"—his iron (and steel) reserve might break.

But I found out that soft stuff alone would never make a general. There comes a time when you need firmness, the iron hand. If I found a general burning his light after hours, with a rug over the fanlight so as to fry sausages for a group of junior officers (as they turned out to be), I never spared him. I'd condemn him to five hundred lines of Virgil as quick as look at him, friend or not. I see the result of it now, though heaven knows I get little credit for it. "General So-and-so," said one of the Sicilian press reports, "can put more into a five hundred word dispatch than any man in the army." Of course he can; he wouldn't waste a word. He counts them as he writes them.

Of another of my generals the press said, "General So-and-so has no knowledge of Italian, but he astonished some of his staff by addressing a few words of well-chosen Latin to a Neopolitan delegation." Yes, but who chose it for him? I did fifty years ago. I chose him the whole first declension (but without the irregular Dative Plural) and the whole of the second declension, including the Vocative Case. He spent all one Saturday afternoon (the incident arose in connection with his having jumped over the school fence on Friday) in writing out these declensions again and again and again. They were the only ones he ever knew. He never went further. And wasn't it lucky? They are the only ones that Southern Italians use anyway! And the Vocative Case, the only one he needed to address them. The papers said it seemed marvellous that he had kept his grip on Latin! So it does, unless he opens up his hand.

So that's the way it went. Steady day-to-day work on these generals gradually taught them duty, self-reliance, the need of a bath once a week, love of country, the folly of jumping fences, the acceptance of discipline and the power of written Latin for the redemption of sin. With that they passed out of my care to what they thought was the beginning of their military life as Cadets in the old "Stone Frigate." But the real beginning, the channel in the sand that later is the fold in the rock, was mine.

All this is true. Yet perhaps I have spoken too much as if I did it all alone. I was reminded of this in receiving a letter the other day from my old friend, Sir Edward Peacock, of London, England. He is now one of the Empire's greatest financiers but in the days of which I speak he was my colleague at Upper Canada College and of no more account in the world than I was—in fact, both nothing. He wrote, "Do you know that you and I taught six of the chief Canadian generals at Upper Canada College?" I have answered, "Take three and give me three; I prefer to keep my staff as a unit."

III

THERE FOLLOW HERE SIX ESSAYS ON THE POST-WAR
WORLD AND SOME OF THE THINGS THAT SHOULD BE
DONE TO ACHIEVE A BETTER PLACE IN WHICH TO LIVE,
ENDING WITH THE SUGGESTION THAT ONE OF THE FIRST
NEEDS IS THAT WE RECONSTRUCT OURSELVES.

This Business of Prophecy

I USED to go in a great deal for prophecy. I found it safer and easier than fact, and more impressive. During my long years of lecturing at McGill I used to say to my classes, "Mark my words, gentlemen, in another fifty years you will see" so and so; or, "Mark me, gentlemen, in another half century you will see the end of" of pretty well everything. The students were tremendously impressed. They didn't see how I could see it all coming. They just lived on the hope of it.

The only mistake was that I made the prophecies too short. They'll soon fall due. I began in 1901, and the first of the prophecies will come around in 1951. It is true that a great many of the older students have dropped out. Even those left begin to look pretty shaky. So I guess it will be all right. Yet it was timed too close. I wouldn't do it again.

But in any case, I have gone out of the prophecy business. Too many people are crowding into it, people without experience. And it is a thing that demands long preparation. Look at those prophets of the Old Testament. They were mature men, 500 to 600 years old, with a bombing range of 3,000 years.

But now everybody's in it. Why, only yesterday at my club a man told me to mark him that the world would be an absolutely different place after the war. I marked him right away (with a piece of billiard chalk) but I doubt if I can find him again—after the war.

That's it, all the time—after the war. They're prophesying and planning all the big things that are going to be done after the war. It seems that the whole framework of society has got to be reconstructed—from top to bottom, or from bottom to top. Some will begin at one end, some the other. Fascinating, isn't it? In fact, some of us can hardly wait till the war is over, and would end it right now so as to get at this post-war stuff. It seems that we've been living in the wrong ideology—I think that's it. Anyway it's all got to change.

Naturally the biggest thing of all is the question of the future of Europe. We have simply got to consider what that is to be. In fact, it is a thing that should have been attended to long ago. Only last week I heard two men discussing quite eagerly, indeed, almost angrily, whether Europe after the war is to be a federation or just a loose conglomerate under a guarantee of conglomeration.

It is a thing you have to face. These two men were going to a meeting (I was so sorry I couldn't go) where they were to thresh this out. They said that after the discussion the future of Europe would probably be thrown open to the audience. That was nice, wasn't it? I forgot to look in the paper to see what happened; often so much war stuff gets into the papers that you miss the news.

But, anyway, what is needed here is one of those big general polls of public opinion that show exactly what is going to be, or, rather, the percentage of everything that is going to be. A lot of us would like to see the future of Europe put to a poll that way, along the lines: (1) Future; (2) no Future; (3) any damn Future. I'll bet you it would show Europe 62 per cent, or say 63, conglomerated. That's what I'd do with it.

Of course there would be the usual 17 per cent "indifferent." Those fellows should keep out of the poll. If they don't care, why do they vote? In fact, the real trouble with these polls is that the very people whose opinions we don't want in the poll are the kind of people who give their opinions, and those we do, don't. Do you see what I mean? If we could get the solid thought of the country to think, it would be better.

But there are big things to plan for at home, too. Take education, one of the biggest. They are saying that after the war education will have to be reconstructed from top to bottom. They say it won't be recognizable. You won't be able to tell whether a man is educated or not. It seems there are a lot of committees, some of the biggest educationalists in the country, sitting on it already. One committee is sitting on arithmetic and working on the multiplication table. They're up to nine times nine already. They may scrap the rest. Another is working on long division; it's too long for them.

But, of course, the biggest post-war thing of all is the reconstruction of the cities. I imagine that that question has come up everywhere. I know that with us in my city it is the most acute problem of all and there's no use ending the war till we solve it. There's no doubt our city has got to go; it's no darned use; the streets all run the wrong way and cross one another. Indeed, the only thing to do with it is to knock it all down and shovel it away.

When I look at my own house, I just want to take a spade and knock it down flat. The thing is worthless; the upstairs ought to be downstairs. Anybody can see that now. And it's the same way with all the apartment buildings. That's the fascination of city planning. You see it all so clearly when you see it. You see, in practically all the apartments the bottom floor should be the top one—to get proper light.

Anyway, in our city we all see eye to eye about it, though in different directions. I see my own house best. However, we've got a committee of experts working on it and they are beginning right at the beginning, at the very foundation of reconstruction—drainage. Are we draining properly? And after that leakage, and then seepage, and then garbage. We had a big man here a week or two back talking garbage. He was certainly right up in it. He's been invited to talk elsewhere. That's the way with these experts; they know their stuff.

But of course it all takes time and spade work. One of our speakers put it pretty neatly the other day by saying you can't rebuild without spade work. That seems to put it in a nutshell, or at any rate in a steam shovel. The only trouble is the time. It would never do to have the war end on us and the city still right here.

Then there's post-war finance—I suppose the nation's greatest problem of the lot. But here the biggest experts, on the biggest salaries, seem to be pretty well agreed: after the war we must keep right on with big expenditure and high salaries for fear of a collapse. It seems that, quite apart from the other Allies, the United States and Great Britain and Canada are spending 365 billion dollars a year. That means a billion dollars a day, and, spread out among the 200 million of us, it means five dollars a day each! I just can't think now how I'll spend mine.

So you see, with all these fascinating post-war problems to think about, you can't blame people if the war news sometimes seems a little dull. There is so much to plan and so little time. I hope those who are fighting won't stop till we get our ideology ready.

Rebuilding the Cities

WAR is a strange business. It does what peace can never effect. The bombing of the great European cities has brought out the fact that they needed bombing anyway. The booksellers of Paternoster Row in London stand among the debris, rubbing their hands to think what a fine book quarter they can make of it now. They expect great things in Bristol, too, though they still need a few edges trimmed off. Similarly we expect to give the Germans a fine chance with Berlin, and the Italians are to have a whole lot of fun with Naples and Genoa.

But with the cities—well, we can all see it so clearly now. They are all wrong. Some are so old and so crooked that you can't move around in them, you can't drain them, you can't light them. Some are so tall and so congested that you can't see out of them and the sun can't get into them. Dr. Alexis Carrel said that soon human beings wouldn't be able to live in New York. I can't already.

All the streets in all the cities are too narrow. Yet the queer thing is they've been making them wider and wider for centuries. When Peter Kalm came to Montreal in 1749, he spoke of the beautiful wide streets—and he meant it—and he was talking of the old French town at that—St. James Street, Notre Dame and St. Paul. They were certainly wide as compared with what he knew in Europe—streets with names that sound like Rue des Anges, Rue des Saints, and in England, Pump Court and Brick Alley.

When Governor Simcoe laid out Yonge Street in Toronto, he made it wide, hopelessly too wide, they said. Go and look at it now. It's that little path that runs north through the middle of the city; look close and you'll see it. Wider and wider they built them; St. Catherine's Road below the Montreal mountain farms was spaciousness itself. Three buggies could pass abreast. The only towns that built streets wide enough were the towns that never grew. I know a place in Missouri—it's called Centre Something—where the street (there is only one) is so wide that it's too wide to cross. People live either on one side or the other. I remember that when I lectured there they asked me which side I'd like to lecture to. The rest of that town is railway tracks, great belts of them. Centre Something doesn't need to rebuild; only to wait.

So there we see already Lesson Number One in city planning. Look far enough ahead; no short sight this time.

But the only trouble is that it is so hard to see what's ahead. Hence what I want to do in this discussion is to show where the difficulties lie rather than to hope to solve them. For example—the first insuperable difficulty—will there be cities at all? Already in England the bombing of industrial cities has led to the decentralization of industry—putting the factories out in the country. Some people are saying that they'll never come back. Why should they? With telephones, everybody can talk to everybody; air travel lands anybody anywhere (or nowhere) in a few minutes; goods and material move more easily in decentralized areas. As to the workers—bring them all along, into new homes, with the breath of the country in the back yards. The first time those fellows see a primrose, they'll go crazy.

So over in England they're saying that the thing to do with the city is to get it out of the city. They imagine a set of centres—semi-rural, semi-industrial, with workers' homes that are little country houses—gardens, rockeries, rookeries—all those things. They even say that the workers who still have to stay in the city for their day's work will prefer to live out in the semi-country anyway.

How like Utopia it sounds!—the city day's work done—and away in a comfortable train—swift as wings, smooth as rubber

—reading the afternoon paper on a wicker seat with lots of room—no standing up and all free, of course, for this is a semi-collectivist state and transport is thrown in, society emancipated from the bottom up.

How brief the trip. Practically not more in time than any ordinary city worker spends today between house and office. I understand that at present the average man puts in seventeen and a half minutes and covers a mile and a quarter. But I don't hold much by that. The "average man" is a poor shrimp; statistics make too much of him. In reality, he has a chest measurement below 37 and never got as far as algebra in school. So we won't reckon by him.

But, as I say, how wonderful this return home after work; the rush for the overalls, the spade, the trout rod, the golf clubs . . .

What the future could be, if we only had the stuff to make it! We certainly need bombing. Drop some more.

But now here is the strange contradiction. We have no sooner visualized these "garden homes for all" in the semi-country than we find that there are plenty of people who won't want them. So it appears from the discussions going on in England—in the papers, I mean. I always take my discussions from England because over there they certainly do discuss things. Here we can't. We're so much alike that we can't discuss. We can only fight. But over there they have different sorts of people who sign themselves "Old Fog" and "late Major, Rawalpindi Field Force, Third Base," and "Workingman"—and so on. We don't have those people here.

So when you ask them where they want to live, you find that there are ever so many who want to live in the city for the sake of the city, the bright lights, the noise, the moving scene about them—it's like a club. So what they are saying over in England is that rebuilding the cities will involve a lot of inner-city housing for those who won't go out. This, I think, is true; it's like being Liberals and Conservatives; people are just that way and can't help it. This question of inner-city versus outer will vary very much from city to city, especially according to climate. In Toronto, people will want to get out as far as they can; in Montreal, they will want to stick inside. They always have.

In my book on Montreal there is a passage which contrasts waiting for a suburban bus on a summer evening in California where young love stands under the magnolia trees hoping the bus will never come, as against waiting in the Montreal suburbs on a February night, thirty below, a blizzard blowing, wind dead astern, for a bus that doesn't come because it's snowed up in Cartierville.

So in such a city as Montreal you must rebuild housing inside the city. You must do it on a giant scale. You must begin by shovelling up flat a huge big area. Shovel the proprietors up with it and throw them into the St. Lawrence. It's quicker than letting crooked proprietors bribe crooked aldermen to cheat the life out of the city by paying too much. I know that just now we have no crooked aldermen left in Montreal. We have councillors now, and they won't even accept salaries. Some one left twenty-five cents on the board room table the other night and it was there in the morning— at least, fifteen cents. But crooked aldermen will come back. They always do, certain as spring.

So look what an appalling difficulty you must face when you begin to plan to rebuild a city; what an avalanche of illicit profits, of crooked bargains, what opportunities for legal theft! Do you know I believe honestly, and I mean it, that we can't plan to rebuild our cities until we first rebuild ourselves. I don't want to talk religion because that's terribly bad taste and very offensive, but somebody has spoken somewhere about renewing a right spirit within us. Till we get it we'd better let the cities alone.

But suppose we get it—or enough of it to make a start. Again we should find a lot of technical difficulties as to what and how to build, and if we rebuild the city wrong again we've wasted another generation. For instance, it is my opinion that the houses of the city of the future will involve certain general principles utterly unknown now. We always think of houses as facing the street. That was nice in the old days. Peter Kalm tells us of how in the old French Montreal of 1749 all the people sat in the evening on their house-steps along St. Paul and Notre Dame Streets, talking and sewing and watching the world go by. But now the world goes by in a cloud of gasoline and a roar of brakes—noise, noise, that never ends. The houses of the coming city will turn their backs on the street—blind walls with doors for garages—and turn their faces inward, locking shoulders around a great inner courtyard, all trees and lawn and flowers. There it is that children will play, young love saunter, and old age doze in the sun.

Community life?—not exactly. Still every man his own, but such a lot for all. . . . We can't tell yet how far life in common will go. Will the people—not that damn average man—I mean ordinary people, want to have community meals in dining halls built into the houses, or will they be like me and want to eat alone, rather cook an egg for myself than share an omelette with a prince—especially with some princes I've seen pictures of . . . ?

No, no—I begin to think that we're not ready to build yet. We don't know enough about it. We've got to *think* some more. You remember how Tennyson wrote in one of his poems, "Consider, William, take a month to think." He had England down pat, didn't he? Well, that's us.

And, anyway, when you come to talk of the housing of the poor, perhaps there won't be any poor! They may slip out on us. So we should perhaps begin by asking them, are they going to stay poor? Because if not, I for one won't spend a lot of money on housing the rich.

Casting Out Animosity

JUST now we are all filled with the idea of post-war reconstruction, rebuilding the railways, recharting the air, shovelling up the cities. I propose, my dear friend, that as a first need for a post-war world you reconstruct yourself a little; shovel up a lot of yourself and throw it away; knock yourself down and start over. And, in particular, cast away a whole lot of minor grievances and mimic animosities that the fierce light of war has brought down to their true pettiness.

The war has shown us what real suffering is, real sorrow, and has revealed the appalling extremity of barbaric cruelty to which human nature can be distorted.

Seen in this light, how petty are the things we used to fuss and quarrel about, how trivial the make-believe animosities that kept people enemies. I have known two professors of Greek who ceased speaking to one another because of divergent views on the pluperfect subjunctive. I've seen lifelong friends drift apart over golf, just because one could play better but the other counted better.

Above all, such animosities arose out of the make-believe of our politics.

I recall from years of long ago two old men whom I knew in the country, bitter partisan opponents. Old Archie hadn't spoken to old Sidney for ten years: no, siree! Archie was a Grit and Sidney was a Tory. You don't know what that means, but then, neither did they. Anyway it kept them apart. There they sat each morning in the "rotunda" of the country tavern (the space between the clerk's desk and the barroom door), waiting for the morning papers from the city off the eleven o'clock train. Each got his paper and started a sideways campaign of sneers, addressed to the room but intended for the other, "I see where some darn fool of a Tory, etc." So it went on for years. Then old Sidney died. I saw old Archie at Sidney's funeral, standing shrunken and silent, his head shaking from side to side. They said that at the next election (his last), he changed his vote.

So while there is yet time, let us realize how petty are these animosities, what good fellows we all are in reality. I recall an English music-hall song with the refrain, "He's all right when you know him, but you've got to know him first." We are all like that. I am sure I am and I think it likely that you are. You may look pretty disagreeable and repellent but that's because you can't help it with that face of yours. Try to let people realize that it is only just your face; that behind it you are all right.

And, mind you, we can do this if we try. For this is exactly what we all do once a year at Christmas: we all pretend to be such good fellows that somehow the whole world looks brighter for the pretence, transformed for twenty-four hours by the merry greetings and the cheery compliments of Christmas.

For you see, it is the illusion that is the real reality. I think that there are only two people who see clearly (at least as to one another), and these are two young lovers, newly fallen in love. They see one another just as they really are, namely, a Knight Errant and a Fairy. But who realizes that that old feller shuffling along in spats is a Knight Errant, too, and that other is a Fairy, that bent old woman knitting in the corner.

This illusion, greater than reality, we grasp easily in the form of what we call art—our books, our plays. We like to read of people in books, better than ourselves. How quickly we respond to them! So, too, with the drama: "All the world's a stage," as Shakespeare said, or at least it could be if we set ourselves to make it so, with each of us idealized into the form of what is really his true self. Come, let us make it so. Let us distribute the parts. Let me see—I'll be the cheery, generous philanthropist—or no, you take that—I'll be the still more cheery fellow, little more than an acquaintance, that he gives the money to. You see, you've heard that I'm hard up (though of course I'm so bright and cheery you'd never guess it) and so you press money on me, or perhaps better, you send me money anonymously; you can start and rehearse it that way at any rate.

And now I'll tell you why I want this reconstruction. It is because I don't believe that we can mend our broken world without it. Treaties and compacts, legislation and pledges, are worthless without the heart and spirit of the people. In the long run, the world can only move with the spirit.

I'm going to start anyway. I'm going to pretend that I'm just the kindliest, friendliest feller that ever stepped along the street. You'll notice it right away when you see me. Only, of course, don't push the thing too far: don't strain it: don't ask me to lend you five dollars on account. Let the mould get set a little firmer first.

And you start, too. Don't wait for the rebuilding of the railways and the recharting of the air and the reorganization of trade with South America and all those things you talk about over a cigar in your armchair. Don't put it up to the President of the United States. You begin.

And when we all get reconstructed—oh, my!—what a bright world! There'll be no trouble then.

Woman's Level

THERE is a very general feeling that after the war women will have the right to be placed on their proper level. We are all for it. The only question is to know where the level is. Do we lift them up to it, or put them down to it, or move them over sideways? In other words, how does woman's level compare with man's level?

This is the question which I wish to discuss. It is very probable that my views will appear to many people quite reactionary. They represent, in part, a reversion to the "home-and-mother" stuff now so widely despised. But in other aspects they run in quite the other direction. At any rate, any one person's views are of interest, if only as a point of departure for wiser people.

The courageous and patriotic service of women in the war has led in certain quarters to the demand for complete equality and uniformity of status of the two sexes. Put in an extreme way, this means that since women can serve as soldiers, then half of the soldiers ought to be women; if women can serve at sea, then half the sailors ought to be women; and similarly half the aviators, half the factory workers, half the miners, half the railway operators and so on. Still more so is it with the white-collar professions. Seen in this light the average banker ought to be half-man and half-woman, the prime minister, as likely as not, an old woman, and the cabinet, by popular vote, a bunch of girls. In setting out to meet an Anglican bishop, one would be prepared to find him an imposing matron in shorts.

One has only to state this half-and-half view of society to show how impossible it is in actual reality, as a basis of human organization. There is a vast section of the activities of men, indeed the larger part of them, from which women are debarred by the initial reason of inferior physical strength. The occupations of war on land and sea and air, the fighting that is called into being by the deplorable necessities of an imperfect world—these must, overwhelmingly, be for men. Even the rougher and heavier tasks of peace, on sea and land, in mines and lumber camps and in the fields, all the *hard* work, must be done by men.

We may call this *hard* work in the simple sense in which chopping wood is hard work and speaking in Parliament is easy. Factories are here a mixed product, with easy work, like that of the general manager, and the "girls on machines," and hard work like that of the furnace men. If any one still doesn't see the difference I want to make as between *hard* work and other work, I can't help him. But the point I want to emphasize is that a great part, a major part, of men's work is *hard* work and that women cannot do it. This means that since the total numbers of the sexes are even, women's main occupations and men's main occupations are by necessity separated. The ground that they occupy in common is only a relatively small part of the field.

This does not deny women the right to do anything that they are able to do. The question of women's rights is a dead issue, a battleground of the past, swept clean by victory and with nothing on it now but monuments—busts of Mrs. Pankhurst, and statues of Carrie Nation and of the other great women who won the cause. All this was a tremendous question in the Nineteenth Century. There is nothing left of it now. In the new world that we are to make after the war, it must be taken for granted that women are to have all the political rights and professional rights that men have—the right to vote on anything and sit on anything that a man can sit on, a size larger if need be.

It seems likely, at least to some of us, that women, on the whole, will make only a very small part of their life out of interest in political activities. Democracy has already shown that even with men most of them don't want to be bothered with active politics, have better things to do (or worse) than to attend trivial meetings and, on the whole, keep away from the control of public affairs. The complexity of our society forces this. Public questions are too intricate in detail for everybody to follow all of them. We are compelled to adopt the process of trying to find a good man who likes that sort of thing and then letting him do it. The obvious danger here is that we are apt to find a bad man. That was why any initial good that there was in Mussolini's Fascism—which meant originally, "let a man rule who knows how"—was lost in its perversion.

Put very simply, this means that women in the new world will keep out of politics. A few will run: a few will sit: a few will talk. They will probably run and talk and sit with about as much, or as little, success as has been already shown by the women who sit and talk and run now. Each of us can judge for himself how great, or small, that success is. But the life and the life work and life interest of future women must lie elsewhere.

So with the professions. Women should have a *right*, and no doubt will have after the war, the right to enter any profession. They will even, let us say, enter the church. To many of us it would seem very strange, even repellent, to "sit under" a woman clergyman preaching from a pulpit. But this is only prejudice, from our upbringing, not reason; and in any case those of us who think this way don't as a rule go to church. So we won't be there. Indeed, it will give us a new reason for staying away.

So with the other professions. Women can be and are doctors—some of them excellent ones. Women can be and are lawyers and judges. But there is not the least danger that either profession, medicine or law, will ever be split up fifty-fifty as between man and woman. It attracts one sex; it does not, except in exceptions, attract the other. Engineering, as practised only by men, is, and must remain, a man's profession, the same as with running saw-logs and pounding sand.

All this, then, is negative, the discussion of what women *won't* do—either can't or won't want to. The real discussion is as to what women in the new world *will* do. I want to show that in my opinion a great part of them, the larger part of them, the most important part of them, will stay at home and raise children, about four children each, statistically, or possibly four and a half. That is what they will do in our country and in similar countries. As to what they will do in India and in the Sahara, I don't know. But in our country, and in similar countries, unless the right women have the right children to about this extent, our national heritage—all that we started from—is not good for a hundred years' purchase.

This contention that the best women ought once again to unite their lives to their homes and children has become so heretical, so offensive to many people, that it requires some hardihood to affirm it, and makes one hasten to explain it. These new homes and mothers will be operating in a world greatly changed from the present world of poverty and slums, of lives on the narrow margin, of apprehension everywhere and security nowhere—the world in which parenthood became a risk undertaken only on a small scale, except by the worst-off classes who could risk everything, having nothing to risk.

The new status of women, then, will be a part of the new world. So we can only understand it by first asking what will this new world be which we are to build up out of the debris of the war. The interest in it does not centre on how to organize it politically. We know all about that. A League of Nations is a Rope of Sand, a Concert of Europe is worse than Grand Opera, and a diplomat is a liar. Our new political world will have all the outward dignity and show of International Leagues, and Committees, and Covenants and Concerts, but all that will be just what the French call *"façade,"* just shop-front. Step inside the shop and there you'll see John Bull and Uncle Sam running the show over a big ledger, with Russia drinking tea (Satisfaction Brand) out of a samovar in an adjoining parlour, and China smoking opium in the corner, all smiles. Out in the Concert Room, there'll be music and refreshments (all free) for the Latin American Nations. The Italians will check the coats.

The real problem will be not the international outlook, but the outlook of the nation inside. For us in Canada the question will be what happens in Canada, not what happens in Germany. There will be those who will see to it that nothing happens in Germany.

Now as to social organization inside. Already there is a certain general consensus about things that must never happen again, and about things to which even the humblest have a birthright. This is focused in a widespread opinion that the world must be made a better place after the war and a widespread determination that it shall be. This is the belief, the hope, the resolve of all truly religious people, of all ardent social reformers, and is the essential creed of all political parties earnest for public welfare. All interests, parties and organizations other than these will go on the scrap heap. The only problem is, to what extent are we to use government action and to what extent are we to trust to individual interest to form our new world? In my own opinion both of them must be used and both must be animated by the spirit of righteousness, without which all government is a choice of tyrannies and all self-interest sinks to rapacity.

The programme thus envisaged has been worked out in general terms to mean that there shall be work and pay for all —decent work and hours of labour, and conditions and pay that permit a decent life of comfort and cultivation, home and shelter for all, care for all in illness and adversity and old age, and, for all, proper holiday vacation and leisure time.

The proof that this is possible is found in the war itself. We look back to the years before the war. What a mockery on our social guidance! What an exhibition of our ignorance and ineptitude! To tell four million people in Britain that there was no work for them, to let twelve million in the United States and half a million in Canada stand idle on the ground that there was nothing to do, that already too much was done; that they must be content with a meagre dole of charity, just enough to keep them from revolt, just enough to keep them alive and breed revolution in their hearts! Now comes war, with food and work and shelter for all, while half, more than half of us, are fighting or contriving death, and all of it taken—where else came it from, than from the annual produce of the nation's work? Don't talk of the people's annual food and clothes and shelter coming out of debt. People don't eat debt, and by debt no coat is made.

All that is plain. Our present question is, where do women come in, in this remade world?

Now here enters another great element of coming social change. The new society will not only alter its way of living but its place of living. A large part of it, probably the larger part, will move out of the "city," as we now know it, to what will be half-city, half-country. This decentralization of industry has already begun in Britain as a safety precaution against bombing. The gregarious human clustering, part instinct, part necessity, that made the congested districts and the slums a blot on our civilization, scattered when the bombs fell. Many will never come back. Our typical factories of the future will be out in the country with very rapid transport at national expense; to every one his home, his "little bit of garden," his "three acres and a cow," that was once the dream of the British artisan. Three acres and a cow! Bread and work for all! How humble were the aspirations of the past.

Not all working people will want to live in the country. In this matter of preference there are two classes of people, those who can't stand the city and those who can't stand the country. There are types of working people, men and women, evolved by two hundred years of factory operation, who prefer at any price, even in mean streets, the bright lights, the noise, the human company of the city, and for whom the open fields and the dull silence and the dark nights of the country breathe monotony and despair. Factory women, we are told, often lost their minds in the early days of prairie settlement.

Some workers therefore will, by choice if not of need, still work and sleep in the big cities. For them, and them only, will survive the "apartment house," the greatest enemy of childhood ever contrived. The stork flies past it, the baby clutched under its wing, looking for a country cottage.

But most people still love the country, and dream of it—at office desks and among the turning wheels of the workroom. That's why rich men go tarpon fishing in Florida; they've gone crazy and think they're in the country; and why poor people crowd in thousands to any cow pasture called a summer park.

Hence, ever so many people will live in the new industrial country centres where babies are as welcome as the flowers of spring, and sit dozing in their sunbonnets in the back gardens.

All social dreamers—and what is better than a dream?—dream of a classless society. I plead guilty to being one of them. Even at its best a class society, one in which there are "gentlemen and ladies" matched off against the "working class," the "common people," the "poor," and "the lower class," et cetera, is a poor business, the worse the more you look at it. For it carries in itself by its lack of opportunity the perpetuation of its sins. In past times it may have seemed necessary, except in a few favoured spots such as Evangeline's Acadia, where "even the richest was poor and the poorest had in abundance." In the past, perhaps it was hard to survive without a class system, and to maintain culture, art and science, except at the price of supporting a privileged few. Even at that one looks back, appalled at the "class" of Victorian England, the easy assumption of merit, the easy tolerance of other people's misery, and the magic lantern of established religion with its peep show for the poor, offering the next world as a substitute for this.

The great legacy given us by the class society is the institution of the domestic servant class. That has got to go. There is no room in our new world for "domestic service" as we knew it in the world that is being ushered out. I have always been surprised how little the women advocates of the emancipation of women have concerned themselves about this. Being mostly women fortunately above the servant class, they have always taken it for granted in their demands for privilege and rights and economic emancipation, that they would have "servants" in their homes. Indeed, their emancipation partly depended on it. But the status of a domestic servant as we have known it—the long indefinite hours, the grudging "evening off," the perpetual menial position—this is not service of a fair contract, this is degradation, just one degree above the domestic slavery which it so closely resembles. If the time comes when all boys and girls are educated up to the age of eighteen, when they all have decent homes (or the chance to make them decent), recreation, the culture of libraries and meetings and social organizations—where among them will you find a "servant"?

In our better world the servant will be replaced by the domestic worker, coming and going under fixed hours, with a status as good as that of—we must not say her "mistress"— let us say with Negro politeness, of the "other lady." In these terms, working as a nurse does, many a girl might prefer paid housework to paid office work, provided the pay and the hours and the status are just as good. Status, you know, is all in your eye. The time was when a "nurse," wet or dry, had the status of Mrs. Gamp. The time was (it seems unbelievable now) when people of quality in England never asked a doctor to dinner. He seemed something like a barber. It's a fact. Read in the latest Victorian biography ("Lord Ponsonby") of how Queen Victoria at last admitted the Balmoral doctor to dine with the quality.

Hence in the destruction of class, many of our views will turn upside down. Girls who finish their education and take up housework will actually seem like educated girls doing housework, and not like servants at all.

In and through all this new complex there will be plenty of women training to be doctors and lawyers and bishops, and running for Parliament; and plenty of women going into offices as girls and staying in business on their own, not as paid employees, but on their own risk and capital, "business women"—as we say "businessmen." These will *seem* plenty if looked at by themselves and added up as a simple total, but will seem very few at all as added up beside all the women in the nation.

What then will ordinary women be doing, after having finished their eighteen years, and perhaps more, of education, and trying two or three years in office work and housework and schoolteaching? The answer is "Home and Mother." They will do this because under the new conditions they will want to. In the society that is coming, all the costs that go with illness and disability will be removed from the individual to the nation at large. Most of all will this be true of all the financial burden that goes with the birth and raising of children. Maternity may have its terrors, but the doctor's bill will not be one of them. Parents will not need to save their pennies to give their children a better education than their own, because they'll get it, anyway; and they'll get all of it, not just part of it, as is given now. Those of us who have dealt with education all our lives know that if you end it at twelve, or fourteen, or even sixteen years of age, you haven't got it all. But you can turn out an educated, cultivated boy or girl of eighteen who has had all the education needed for life, liberty and the pursuit of happiness; a girl fit to talk to, and a boy fit to talk about. On top of that, college represents merely the special turn of the general road that leads into particular alleys.

College is grand for those for whom it is grand: unnecessary for others, provided they all had the real thing up to eighteen years of age. College education for girls, it seems to me, has been vastly overdone. They crowd into it in thousands, having nowhere else to crowd into; then are turned out at the other end of it to crowd into schoolteaching in numbers that keep swamping the profession. Schoolteaching is properly a profession for old men. The only schoolmaster figures I can idealize are those of the old Scottish dominie, devoted and self-important, and Monsieur Hamel of Daudet's pathetic story of the Last Class (the last class taught in French in Alsace in 1871), and Mr. Chips dying over tea and toast after sixty years of service.

Girls went to college and then to teaching because—it is a simple truth—office work was for years thought beneath them and only now is being made good enough for them. In reality, office work, beginning with a mere routine but advancing to a position of trust and responsibility, offers a girl a better salary, better conditions and a more interesting life than most schoolteaching does. Fetch the old dominie back; dust him off and prop him up in his chair again.

We are saying, then, that the financial burden of maternity and the costs of children's education—the whole of it, a clear eighteen years of it—will be all gone. Even the maintenance of the children at home during their years of education will be, of necessity, in part defrayed by the government. A married woman with children must draw a government salary for being a married woman with children, just as at present an old maid, an *old* one, without children, draws a salary for being an old maid without children.

In that case, what is to stop early and easy marriage, as fresh and free and willing as the war marriages that blossom out like flowers to brighten the wasted field of war? Why not marry and why not have children? Why not that little sub-suburban cottage, among the love bees, with the baby in the sunbonnet in a perambulator in the back garden, chuckling at father's attempts to plant beans?

The rearing of children in a house fit to rear them in, not an apartment house, is a full-time job, but it is one that we have to get done for us somehow, or else our nation, all that is best in it, and our civilization, all that holds it, must go under within a hundred years. We have got to have the right people brought into the world, our world. The right people to keep the world safe and decent and fair, for all the people, decent or not, are the English-speaking peoples. These are mainly in the British Empire and in the United States. And the really right part of them, the part that animates and inspires all the others, are the people in Britain, in British countries and in the United States—of British stock and traditions and institutions.

These are our own people irrespective of political boundaries. With these are closely associated people of such kindred descent, traditions and ideas—the Scandinavians and the Dutch—that their families amalgamated with ours and became of one blood. Call this stock British, remembering that it includes the United States, and the meaning is clear. With this stock goes for us in Canada the fixed bloc of French Canada, in no danger of racial diminution. But in Canada, unless we maintain this British stock, we are lost. For the truth is that, relatively, this British stock has been weakening for two generations. The birth rate has fallen low among the people with whom we most need it high. Migration has replaced the birth of new children, and not the old-fashioned migration of early days, the incoming of British people to a British colony, but a polyglot migration out of Central Europe. Nothing can restore the balance except children and more children. North America can easily take in two million people a year and we need them all British. And when they come they must bring their own stork with them.

That is how I see the situation of women in North America. But I am trying to present this status of women in our nation of tomorrow, not as what women ought to do, but as what women are going to do, what they *want* to do if they get a chance. After all what better in the long run? People who have never married have not really lived. People who have married and had no children have only half-lived. People who have one child only are a long way from the crown of human life. Old age with nothing to look back upon, nothing to lean upon, is poor stuff as compared with the old age that renews its youth and life and interests in its children and grandchildren. Ask a few lonely old people going out with the tide.

The School Is the Lever

ARCHIMEDES once said, "Give me a lever long enough, and a fulcrum strong enough, and single-handed I can move the world."

We have come to a time when we want to move the whole world, to make it socially better. And I know of a lever that we can use to move it—the school.

Everybody knows that there has gone abroad all over the face of the world a determination to make the world a better place to live in, to abolish the poverty and want. The war has revealed that this place is possible. It has shown us the enormous power of co-ordinated production. We must turn this vast mechanism of death into the maintenance of life.

But how do we begin? If we want to make a new people, we find that most of us, all but the very young, are already unfitted for the new "class-less" world of our dreams. Some of us had no chance. Some had too much. For some of the brightest minds the doors of school closed with childhood. A life of overwork and under-holidays has battered most people out of their true shape. There is little to love in them at sight, but we can read the meaning that lies in the face that's all wrinkled with furrows and care.

So we must begin with the children, the school. We must have real schools that mean a beginning of life to the point where an assured step may be taken on firm ground—till a boy of eighteen can say with pride and confidence, "Now, I'm ready. Leave the rest to me."

School education should go on till it's *finished*. Any teacher knows what I mean. It should carry on till it has given a mental training and imparted an orbit of information that is sufficient for the work and leisure of life. College training is a special thing. It is or should be only for specialized purposes of distinct professions or for research and further scholarship or for teaching. The kind of general slush given as general courses for students at college, starting with no purpose and heading nowhere, is about as nourishing as bran mash. You might as well put a poultice on their feet.

But a real education can be given to boys and girls and be finished at the age of eighteen, provided they are set free from all other work and have all the proper facilities. And this means a long step more than mere teaching. It means medical care, the cult of fresh air and exercise, the use of leisure, the pleasure of entertainment. It should mean free books given forever to any boy or girl who has earned them with recitations and to be carried away later and kept as trophies of school, as little Iroquois learned to keep a scalp.

I would go further. I would supply school meals, of which one, the midday meal, would be eaten, by custom, in common by the rich and the poor. It would not be "the thing" for rich parents to keep their children from it. I would go as far as I could with the giving of school clothes to poorer children, given somehow, if one could, to avoid the hurt feelings of a charity gift—and if possible I would obliterate, at least for a few short hours of school, the social differences of the home. I often think of the good old college gown which was discarded all too stupidly here in Canada at the bidding of foolish people who confounded aristocracy with antiquity and lost from sight the original purposes of the things they threw aside. The college gown covered, for the poorer ones among us, a multitude of patches and made us all, as we sat on the benches of the college of sixty years ago, as equal each to each as triangles in Euclid.

If I were King—as they used to say—or if I were society at large—I would give all this, education, health and sunshine, up to the age of eighteen or so—and then I would say to the world:

"Now! Look at these. Try to crush these down to your 'working class' or 'proletariat'! Try to house these in slums or cast them out into unemployment! You can't do it. The world is theirs."

But it is time to begin. It may be later than we think.

To Every Child

MISERY breeds war.

You can never have international peace as long as you have national poverty.

You may multiply the pomp of the parade grand as you will, but if behind it is the festering slum, war will come as certain as the spread of pestilence.

What I mean in a plain way is that we must enter on a vast, titanic struggle against poverty and want. What we United Nations did in war we must do in peace, the same union of hearts, the same purpose for all.

This must be the work of the Spirit, not of line and rule and document.

Each of us must stand appalled at the further existence, after the war of misery and poverty, of lives frustrated by want, of children underfed, of people sunk from their birth below a chance to live. We must decide that that must not be, just as we decided that savage conquest and brutality should not be.

To effect this we must unlearn our economics, scrap the whole of it. I have, personally, fifty years of it to throw away!

The fault with economics was the assumption that what *can only be done by the Spirit* could be done by material interest. . . . Business had done much for mankind; but society won't hold together on a business basis alone. . . . Nor on any basis which excludes the animating Spirit of the common man.

There is no fear that the world will not easily support us all. A family may be crowded, but a nation never. The old

Malthusian doctrine of overpopulation as preventing social happiness, of the poor dying as the buffer to save the rich, is all gone. Did it ever convince any one? Even Malthus married and was a father.

Especially with the children lies our chief chance. Older people are battered out of shape, or were never battered into it. Faces all wrinkled and furrowed with care cannot be altered now. But to every child we must give the chance to live, to learn, to love.

Nor does social regeneration mean the obliteration of individual life. The roots lie too deep. There are limits to the amalgamation of society to the common employment of everything by everybody. One's own is own's own. Many of us would rather have a house all our own in the bush than share a palace with a prince—especially with some of them.

We can have a League of Nations if we like. If we do it will be a consequence, not a cause. Thus will come International Harmony—by not looking for it. So it is with life. Try to buy happiness, by the quart or by the yard, and you never find it. Motion it away from you while you turn to Duty and you will find it waiting beside your chair. So with Good Will on Earth. Cannons frighten it. Treaties fetter it. *The Spirit brings it.*

IV

STEPHEN LEACOCK'S REPUTATION AS A HUMOURIST
WAS EQUALLED BY HIS ABILITY AS AN ECONOMIST. ONE
SUBJECT ON WHICH HE WROTE WITH AUTHORITY WAS
THAT OF THE GOLD STANDARD. HERE AGAIN THE SUB-
JECT, WITH ALL ITS INTRICACIES, WAS PRESENTED IN
A VERY READABLE MANNER, WITH EVEN A LAUGH NOW
AND THEN.

Gold

I⊤ has been wittily said—indeed, I may have said it myself—
that there are three great questions that practically never
leave us: the Woman Problem, the Drink Problem and the
Gold Problem. In wartime these questions fall silent, but
with the first return of peace their voice is heard again. Those
who had occasion to follow the economic discussions which
arose immediately after 1918 will remember that the question
of the return to the gold standard was among the first of them.
The decision given was that the gold standard, in the words
of Professor (now Lord) Keynes, was as "antiquated as the
stagecoach" and that what was needed was a "managed currency." Managing a currency proved to be like managing a
bronco. It flew off in all directions. Currencies expanded,
exploded, inflated: marks turned to gas and francs to tears;
bad money beat out good and the worse the money the
better the export trade. The world was still living in a chaos
of broken currencies, tied up here and there with string, when
the present war washed them all up on shore as wreckage.

So now the world must begin again. It is one of the first
signs of returning peace that the money question, the gold
question, is up again. But this time the wheel has turned
a full circle; the demand is now not for managed paper but
for solid gold; not to ride the whirlwind but to sit on something you can feel under you. Hence the new demand for
gold. Lord Keynes, when he was a professor, was content
with an idea. Now that he is a lord he thinks like a lord,
and wants something solid, no new gimcrack idea about it,
something with class and antiquity behind it—in short, gold.
The other experts also return to their first love. In vain they

pretend it's another girl. The attractive Miss Unita is really the same as the solid Miss Pound Sterling of Queen Victoria's time.

With us in Canada this problem has a double interest. It concerns us, along with three or four other countries, as producers of gold. It also concerns us, along with all the world (or all that counts), as a community using a money standard. Let us begin with the purely monetary aspect.

And here I may be pardoned if I give a brief explanation of the once familiar theory of the gold standard. It is less familiar now even among bankers. Some of them, let us say, among the readers of this article are so young that they never knew it; others so old that they've forgotten it. It was one of those great simple truths, never to be contradicted or altered, that were characteristic of the Victorian era which began before Queen Victoria was born and lasted till after she was dead. These truths covered all heaven and earth, yet were so simply expounded that the great Victorian theorists could step on the platform and explain each one as easily as a conjurer doing a turn. Here was Mr. John Stuart Mill taking Free Trade out of a hat, out of any hat— pass it up from the audience! foreigners invited. Here was Professor Huxley with his Atom in a bowl of water; and best of all was Professor Herbert Spencer with his turn on God, Immortality and the Soul. He simply rolled on the stage a little black cabinet, with the word UNKNOWABLE in white capital letters across it. Then he bowed to the audience and said, "Ladies and Gentlemen, they're inside the cabinet," and rolled it off the stage again. After that the audience never need think of it again as long as they lived, in fact not till right on their deathbed. Best of all was the big comic turn called International Law, or Abdul Asiz and As Wuz, with the Sultan of Turkey in it as the Juvenile Delinquent. It was played three hundred times a year for thirty years—as part of the Concert of Europe.

Such was the turn called Standing Up the Gold Standard.

Watch it close. Try to see where the trick comes in. I'll roll
my sleeves up before I write it. Now—

With absolutely free competition, all things offered for
sale tend to exchange just in proportion to the amount of
labour and capital used to make them. Any shift that puts
them out of this proportion must induce people to make
extra ones, or lead them to cut off some of the making.
Gold is just a commodity. It is got by putting labour and
capital into mining. If it takes about as much labour and
capital to produce a bushel (60 lbs.) of wheat as it does to
produce 23 odd grains of gold, then that's what a bushel
will exchange for. If you like to stamp the 23 grains into
a coin and call it a dollar, that makes everything convenient
but doesn't in the least affect how much the dollar will buy.
That depends, as we said, on the cost of production. If you
strike a place like California in 1849, where you pick up
gold in every river bed but where there is hardly a hen in
sight, then people will give (did give) a dollar for an egg.
But that only sent a forced draught of hens into California—
indeed, of all commodities!—and set up railroad building to
carry them till the level of prices and production came smooth
again, like water in connected reservoirs.

"Coins" of gold were just bits of certified gold—the name
didn't matter, nor the government, except to guarantee hon-
esty. Pounds, roubles, dollars, francs—they all had a straight
percentage relation according to the gold in them, the "mint
par of exchange" they called it. The names were as varied,
the units as confused as antiquity itself, but you turned
them all, as they did, into percentages of the British pound
or penny—not the U. S. dollar—and thus got your table:
New York, 4.86⅔; Paris, 25.221; St. Petersburg, 9.46, etc.
Some countries used silver: that meant a little extra arithmetic and a double fluctuation like riding two circus horses;
some countries ran out of gold (as did Italy) and had to use
irredeemable paper. That was like falling off the circus horse.
It ranked along with chronic drink and infidelity.

So that's how the thing worked. A London merchant bought American goods, and sent across gold—any kind of gold. Actually, they went on sending gold coins of dead monarchies and faces of forgotten emperors. It didn't matter. All was gold that glittered. But, as a matter of fact (as any bright boy in the class guessed), they soon found—well, soon? they were British, call it half a century; at any rate, they knew it before the American Revolution—that they didn't need to send the pay for each purchase by itself, but only *balances:* and as banks grew and large finances—not even balances, or not all the time—they just shoved it all forward till trade crowded one way too much and then they sent gold. After each American harvest, gold came as a sort of backwash over the ocean.

That meant, if you think of it, that prices had to keep at the same or something like the same level in all countries. Otherwise, if gold would buy more in one country than in another, then all the gold would go there to buy things instead of buying them at home. . . . Yes, but here was the joke—in proportion as gold piled up in any one country the very piling up made it, so to speak, redundant, and people gave more and more for it; in other words, prices went up, the place ceased to be a good place to buy in and the process corrected itself. It was an automatic regulation. Any stage economist could explain it with hardly any apparatus— just a dollar and a few simple properties. In fact, he'd do it for fifty cents.

No deception so far, is there?

Observe, we said, prices would remain—pretty even, not absolutely even. Of course there were temporary ups and downs (tending to come level, like shaken water in a bath) or ups and downs due to fixed circumstances; things like permanently difficult transport—a piano in the Himalayas must cost more than a piano in Calcutta, and one in Calcutta more than one in London; differences, too, in prices of labour and services, corresponding to differences of race and habit or to lack of mobility. A Portuguese East African Negro would work for two cents a day, if he worked at all, because if he saved up five dollars he could buy an extra wife and never work again. It's pretty hard to turn that into what is called "pure economics," isn't it? That doesn't quite fit into St. James Street, Montreal (they might do something with it on Wall Street). But all those things were put by the economists into a little cabinet called "Friction" and wheeled off the stage.

They had another little cabinet called "Obstruction," and that meant things like a protective tariff, or labour unions for high wages. But those things only made a sort of hump in the ground: the level was still there, the whole surface of the economic world being as smooth there in regard to gold as the surface of a billiard ball. Physically it is. The average height of any spot on earth is about a quarter of a mile (or less) above the level of the sea. The diameter of the earth is 8,000 miles: approximately 500,000,000 inches. On the same scale, the surface of a billiard ball (diameter two inches) would only have a variation of .000006 inches. You'd hardly find your shot disturbed by that: so with the free trade shot down the table. . . .

Still no deception?

Just one other important thing. The production and supply of gold is really not entirely like that of wheat and boots and shoes, ordinary commodities: these are produced and consumed each year, or within a short time. Gold remains. The supply, except for the small loss of shipwreck, etc., is always there. The new supply only adds to it. But this, says the economist on the stage, only makes it more stable. A sudden boost of annual production only lifts the total stock a little. The new California gold lifted prices a little, so did South Africa . . . but not more than the lift effected by an annual output on a supply twenty-five times as great as itself.

The question then arises as to what could break down the gold standard? The answer is that, as with the whole framework of banking institutions, it must break at any time if everybody stood on it all at once. If all creditors everywhere, or even most creditors, or even a whole lot of creditors, called for gold payment, the standard would break. So it would again. But that is nothing. That only means that all the gold in the world is as nothing beside all the payments due. The only significance is that, of course, any return to the gold standard must imply a certain general confidence, a certain general consensus. A scramble for gold could break it. Note, however, that for Great Britain it never broke from 1819 to 1914.

The outbreak of the Great War of 1914 snapped the bonds of the gold standard like thread. The sudden demand for payments in London drove exchange in New York up to $6 a sovereign, there being no time to send actual gold over. Later on, the need for payments in the United States (war material) drove the exchange value of the sovereign down to $3.50. The "gold points" (limits of fluctuations made by actual shipment) vanished and never came back. Restrictive law forbade export and import. The gold standard, as they say in Yiddish, was "all." Britain and the United States and Canada all managed to keep their currencies, depreciated in purchasing power as shown by the three-to-one prices of 1920, but still a going concern. European currencies blew up; the mark cleverly expanded by a million to one, and then to far more, dissolved into gas with a laugh on foreign bondholders; the franc fell till prices were four to one—observe, nicely enough to starve poor people on fixed incomes (as it did), not enough for a new start all around. In Central Europe the confusion of exchange blocked trade. As Fascist Italy and Nazi Germany arose, currency was clamped into the same iron frame as the rest of industrial life. John Bull and Uncle Sam staggered along, arm in arm, going somewhere, drunk. Their satellite children they housed for safety in apartments called the Sterling Block and the Dollar Block, warned not to go out.

But before discussing that, I turn a moment to the other side of the interest of Canada in gold, its production in the Dominion.

The world's gold, before the present war, was produced mainly by four chief countries, South Africa, the United States, Canada and Soviet Russia. Of these, South Africa was the most vitally interested. What was to the United States a very minor industry meant for the Union the basis of its economic life. Gold in South America meant about 90 per cent of its mineral production, 70 per cent of its export (with no other considerable items beyond wool and diamonds), and equalled about one-half of the gross value of all its manufactured products. What wheat is to Saskatchewan, gold is to South Africa.

This is not just an item of curious interest to put in an almanac. It is a vital basis of world policy, since Great Britain could never "let South Africa down" by adopting a policy which meant casting out gold. This is not philanthropy. Financial South Africa lives on Lombard Street and holds "kaffirs."

Canada before the war had risen from no place at all to competition with the United States for second place, producing about 13 per cent of the world's gold. The mining of gold represented in Canada $205,789,000 in 1941, as compared with agriculture's $1,379,386,000. There is every likelihood that Canada will become the world's chief producer. South African gold is limited to one huge hump in the ground (Witwaters Rand), forty or fifty miles long. The Canadian gold fields are spread all around the Laurentian Shield that encircles Hudson Bay and begin again in the Mackenzie Basin and start over again beyond the Rockies.

Gold production in Canada, from the opening of the northern mining fields, went steadily forward till the break in 1942. Before the Great War it had reached, in 1913, a total of 802,793 fine ounces, valued at $16,598,923; at the onset of the depression (1930) a total of 2,102,168 fine ounces, valued at $43,453,601, and in the last year of the peace (1938) the figures stood at 4,725,117 fine ounces, valued at $166,205,990. The value after 1931 had shifted from a rate of $20.67 an ounce to a rate of $35 U. S. ($38.50 Canadian) which further swells the total. Production in 1940 was 5,332,857 ounces, valued at $204,925,995.

The production of 1941 as a total surpassed all previous records with 5,345,179 fine ounces, valued at $205,789,392. But the increase was only in Quebec, Saskatchewan and the Northwest Territories, and offset a decline elsewhere. The case of the Territories is notable. Here the total of 77,354 fine ounces represents a 40 per cent increase over the previous year.

It is of great importance to note the distinction of the so-called "straight gold mines" in which gold is the sole, or practically the sole product, and the "copper-silver-gold mines" in which gold is a secondary or even a by-product. Contrast here the mines of the Porcupine district, the Hollinger and such, which are "gold mines," with the Flin-Flon mines which are gold-silver-zinc-copper and other mixed mines. The "gold mines" greatly predominate in production. In Quebec they represent, in the form of twenty-three producing mines, about 77 per cent of output; in Ontario still more. The latest statistics (1941) show 82.66 per cent of Canadian production as from the gold bullion bars produced at "gold mines"; 10.23 per cent from blister or anode copper; 4.68 per cent from copper-nickel matte, ores, slag, etc.; 1.99 per cent from alluvial gold and 0.39 per cent from base bullion made chiefly from silver-lead ores.

The important bearing of this is that it shows that closing the "gold mines" means practically closing the industry. Gold can not function as a by-product.

Since the departure from the gold standard and the prohibition of private ownership, gold produced in Canada is bought by the government at a fixed price of $35 U. S.

currency, plus a premium, to make $38.50 in Canadian funds. Theoretically, the Canadian dollar is still based on $20.67 to one fine ounce, no longer the nominal standard of the United States.

As the pressure of the present war grew heavier on our industrial life, a new situation developed in regard to the mining of gold. It became clear that we must turn all industrial effort away from non-essential production. It was the failure to do so that "bust" the monetary system in the Great War of 1914-1918. People who draw high wages and then call for gramophones, spring hats, new motor cars, and new overcoats, boost the manufacture of luxuries, squeeze production till there's not enough of anything, and up goes the Spiral of Prices like a Genie of Smoke out of the bottle in the Arabian tale. The whole plan of the world economy, as taught before the war by English economists like Geoffrey Crowther, with our Mr. Ilsley as the bright boy at the top of the class, rests on curtailing production: on giving the workers lots of money and nothing to buy: and keeping them all dressed up (in their old clothes) and nowhere to go. Seen in a bird's-eye view from above, it's perfectly simple: you look down and see people making and consuming nothing but what war demands—food, gunpowder, transport. The only trouble is that so few of us are birds.

Now—it is clear as mud—producing gold in Canada is of no service in winning the war, with an ally holding—what is it?—$20,000,000,000 of it at Fort Knox in Tennessee. To dig out gold in North Ontario and dig it in, in Tennessee, is on the face of it idiocy. Luckily for our gold producers, many of them are producing other metals, the very sinews of war, and can't help producing gold as a part-product or even a mere by-product. But others, like the mines in the Kirkland Lake and Timmins fields, produce nothing else. Each one of these districts is a little South Africa. Gold is its life. Here you have in and around Timmins over forty thousand people all dependent on gold.

Hence when the government undertook (1941-1942)—and I think quite rightly—to restrict the production of gold by various regulations regarding labour supply, new development, import of machinery, etc., there was an immediate outcry. A delegation went up from Timmins to Ottawa— or is it down to Ottawa—up and down, both, eh?—thank you—and received the usual lullaby answer. Undoubtedly the delegation was right. So was the government. But the solution doesn't lie in letting Timmins produce gold but in giving it a chance to produce, or do something else at just as good pay. . . .

Yet certain people, and among them so high an authority as the veteran geologist, Dr. J. B. Tyrrell, sounded a note of alarm at any restriction of gold, arguing that we need it all.

All that, however, is just our national aspect of the question. There is no doubt of the interest of Canada in gold. It goes far beyond anything that can be shown by statistics. It supplies the incentive—*aura sacra fames*, the cursed lust of gold—that opens up the waste spaces of the earth and turns private greed to a public benefit.

But what about the world at large? Will gold remain after the war as an essential part of the world's economy? There is every present symptom that it will, or at least that if it doesn't, it won't be for lack of trying. The temptation to say, "I told you so," is difficult to resist in youth, impossible to restrain in old age. So I will not try to restrain it. I am glad to think that I advocated a return to the gold standard even in the dark days when Professor Keynes said that the gold standard had gone the way of the stagecoach. The mistake which I made along with so many other people was that I did not realize that the attempt, twenty years ago, to set up the gold standard at the same old mint content of the pound and dollar as had prevailed till 1914 would mean, of necessity, a fall in prices that would depress business and create unemployment.

But a return to the gold standard does not necessarily mean

the return to a pound sterling containing the former number of grains of pure gold. Indeed, the United States has already (1934), through the authorized actions of the President, declared a dollar to mean 13.71 grains of pure gold in place of the previous 23.22. It is true there is as yet no such coin and no such coinage.

It is obvious that in starting the new system the mint content of the coin (if coins are used), or of the monetary unit, must be carefully adjusted. The thing called a dollar should represent the amount of gold that would in a free market be bought with a dollar. On this plan the original U. S. Coinage Act of 1792 initiated the American gold and silver dollars. The British Units never began; they just grew up. And there is now no free market. We don't know how many ounces of gold a dollar would buy. Purchase is all statutory and fixed.

What has happened, apparently, is that in both Great Britain and America there has arisen a profound distrust of the purely abstract standard of value (a mathematical conception based on average of prices). Hence both the British plan submitted by Lord Keynes and the American plan submitted to the President contemplate a banking and paper money currency for daily use, with a solid basis of gold—under it or behind it, or beside it—they are not exactly certain which. The American plan names a unit to be called a *Unita*, taken from the United Nations. The name is not so new as they think (or perhaps they don't think). The *Unite* (meaning United Nations, England and Scotland) was the chief gold coin in England from the accession of James I to the Restoration of 1660.

The English plan suggests a unit to be called a "bancor" which is in some way to be based on actual gold.

Most of the actual gold bullion in the world is, as said, in the possession of the United States. It is of no physical service and to lend it to the outside world that needs reconstruction would seem like getting something for nothing. So it would be. If the United States lent to Greece a billion actual dollars (a hundred million Unitas), and the same to Denmark, Holland, Norway and all the decent, trampled-down and bankrupt nations, they could then, each of them, start up a banking and paper note currency in the good old-fashioned way, and everybody trade with everybody as merrily as in Mid-Victorian days. You may add to this a general superbank (in London or New York)—not surrounded by dens of thieves like the pitiful Bank of International Settlement still existing in Switzerland for the benefit of Germans. The Dutch and other reserves could be focused at London and hence make the total go further, carry a bigger per cent of the load of paper deposits, as easily as a Zulu woman carries a clothesbasket on her head.

Here are the questions that arise: Will the system work of itself? Or do you have to work it? Does everybody have to promise to play fair? Or does it work like Adam Smith's automatic world in which everybody consulted his own interest and so advanced that of everybody else?

For example, suppose the United States by means of high tariffs and such practices shut out European goods, and when they sold to Europe new motor cars and machinery, took payment only in gold; would that mean that the gold would all, or a lot of it, drift back to Tennessee? Presumably it would. In a large sense the United States would have given to the European world a lot of excellent motor cars and machinery for nothing. It is generally understood that the Americans have sworn off this one-sided trade, as a drunkard swears off drink. Question, can they keep to it? Or will Uncle Sam take just one little nip out of the Protectionist bottle, and then just another, and a chaser . . . And won't some people say that it does him good? If people in the dark places of the newfangled world are going to work at starvation wages, will you buy what they make and force our own labour to go idle or work cheap? Take Japan: if, after the peace, the dirty little pups work half-starved, who cares? Will you sell to them? Certainly, for gold. Buy from them? Never! . . .

Moves up from Japan to India, then to depressed Europe. The problem gets harder as you go. I make no pretence of solving it. I consider the world factors too complicated, the economic gears too intricate for any prophecy about the operation of a gold standard in connection with the backwash of gold to the United States. But this much is true: it is better to accept a chance of success than fall back on a certainty of failure. This failure would result, I am certain, from any attempt to run the commerce of a post-war world on a chaos of national currencies with no fixed interlocking of one with the other.

A further difficulty remains. Is it intended that currencies are actually redeemable, day by day, dollar by dollar, from the Unitas to paper, from papers to bancors? That's the crucial question in the construction of the mechanism. That was the essence of the gold standard. Nor can we dodge the question: either money is redeemable, free to come and go, import and export, or it isn't. It is impossible, indeed, to restrict redemption to large sums, and to confine it to central places. But either you redeem it, or you don't. My opinion is that you must—redeem and redeem till you have no gold left—and then put up the sign, "Yes, we have no Unitas."

How will prices act, with a redeemable monetary system? In my opinion, prices will not be much influenced by the annual production, more or less, of gold. The equation is buried too deep. When the output of California and Australia began, a world production of $100,000,000 a year (old scale $20.67 per fine oz.) was added to a world stock of $2,500,000,000. Yet prices, though they rose, did not rise in any dangerous way. At present a world annual production of 40,000,000 fine ounces ($800,000,000 old scales) would be added to an existing stock of $28,000,000,000. It won't affect general prices in any way that can be distinguished from more direct and active factors. The fluctuation will be in mining profits, in the closing and reopening of gold mines in response to the rise and fall of wages, due to other things.

In any new world that we can think of, prices will be far more controlled than they used to be forty years ago. Economic complexity demands it, and war experience shows that it can be done. But this control will be like a tension over the surface, not reaching down to the depths, waves in the sunlight that leave the deep water undisturbed.

What I am advocating, in plain words, is the gold standard; not part of it, all of it. Take all the gold there is. Lend it around among our friends: get the bank signs painted: then shout, "Go!"

Can We Beat Inflation?

EVERY age and generation has its special mysteries, its special terrors, its special realms of fear. It fears vague dangers that drive it to blind frenzies—witchcraft, the coming of the Turks or the approach of the end of the world.

And for each generation the terrors of the ones that preceded it seem absurd and even laughable. There was a time in the Sixteen Hundreds in Europe when all the people gathered, each night for weeks, in the churches praying God to take away "The Comet." It was getting bigger every night with a tail of fire halfway across the sky. And to think that it was just dear old "Halley's Comet," friendly as Mary's Lamb, and back on its last visit in 1910. For quite a time the prayer books of the Church of England printed in the Litany, "From the Turk and from the Comet, Good Lord, deliver us." If you don't believe it, ask any clergyman of the Episcopal Church. He won't know, but you can ask him. "The Turk" was another terror going strong at the time.

Or much later than that, right down in the Nineteenth Century, in the United States itself, people used to get sudden waves of fear that the world was coming to an end. The terror was worked this way: First you formed a "Sect." A sect was as easy to start in an American backwoods town of 1840, like Pittsburgh or Chicago, as it is to start a steelmakers' union today. Then the sect started a rumour that the world was coming to an end. Then they named the actual day, and terror swept the back settlements. The people would gather, quaking, on the hilltops on a summer evening to see the world end. It didn't.

This happened not once but several times. In fact there

was great relief when Lord Kelvin, the Great—whatever he was great at—announced that the earth was good for a billion years. Short as it sounds today, it was a relief.

Well, the point is that in the throes of war and national danger we have picked up our own particular terror, the bogey of today—the Inflation of the Currency. We are not scared of Japs or Germans, but at the word "Inflation" we quiver with fear, shake with rage and reach out for an axe.

You recall the old Arabian Fable of the Genie in the Bottle. Here you had a powerful evil spirit corked up in a bottle. You could let him out if you simply pulled the cork, and he'd promise to be your servant if you did. And mind you he had tremendous power—money, wealth, jewels—those things were as pebbles to him. But if you did let him out, the Genie then would expand and grow and swell into a great black spiral cloud that darkened the whole sky . . . and the cloud then turned to a vast dark form with outstretched, clutching hands, ready to hurl you into black destruction. What good your petty jewels then?

Our Genie in the Bottle is Inflation. And you notice that awful "spiral" form taken over straight from the fable and appearing as the "vicious spiral." People who have no idea what a vicious spiral is, warn us against it. Get that "vicious spiral" into the currency and up it goes, away, away up like the vicious boy in Excelsior.

What I am trying to say is that the new terror is becoming largely just terror without any clear idea of what it really is. When we hear that the steelmakers of Pittsburgh want another eighty cents a minute (or is it a second?), we shake our heads apprehensively. We don't grudge the eighty cents: but the currency? If those fellows keep on they'll inflate it. And not only steelmakers, not only the big things, but even in the ordinary small business of daily life. If a corner grocer inflates eggs from forty to forty-five cents, there's a feeling that he may be starting a vicious spiral right here in our own town.

People make this mystery all the more mysterious because men, most men, pretend to understand all about it, and women, most women, pretend to understand nothing about it. That is their attitude in general about economics. "I don't profess to understand economics," says a woman, meaning, "so much the worse for economics." "It's just a plain matter of economics," says the man, meaning, "that's my affair."

So let us try to get light. What is inflation? What is a vicious spiral? Is there a danger? Can we get out of it?

The answer I want to arrive at—but not too soon—let's have a little fun with it first—is: yes, there *is* inflation; and there *is* a spiral; and it *is* a real danger; and it has in the past, again and again, led to collapse and disaster and stagnation. But we can avoid it as easily as a lion tamer walks around in a lion's cage, or an electrician handles forty thousand volts of electricity. Just exactly as easily as that.

Now let us turn back—economics always has to—if it is only just a few centuries for a few minutes.

Currency began with any common thing that primitive people traded around because it was always good for something. Eskimos used fishhooks. In Kurdistan the Kurds used goats as currency. Where is Kurdistan? It's where the Kurds kept goats. Inflation began in Kurdistan. Starting goats as currency led to such prosperity that the goats bred so fast that it inflated the currency, stopped trade and plunged them in adversity.

The nations learned to use chunks of gold and silver as currency. These couldn't increase. There was just so much. That plan lasted two thousand five hundred years, from the first coins in Asia Minor, 1000 B.C. to the discovery of America. Gold and silver currency worked all right but oh, how feebly. There was so little of it and that little, by loss, kept getting less. You recall the good Samaritan in the Bible who said, "Look after this poor man: clothe him, feed him and keep him till I come. Here's two cents, and if it runs to more than that let me know."

Gold and silver from America came, says history, "in a flood." Not really; that's just "history." All the gold from Mexico and Peru in a year was about one thirtieth of the year's crop of New Ontario and New Quebec. But it was enough to flood the Europe of that day. People offered so much of it, so readily, that up went prices (1500-1600), three to one, but oh, so slowly. It took three lifetimes. All the way from 1600 to 1800, prices went up but not too fast, because "business" (volume of transactions) went up as fast or faster. So the world went very well then, as an old song had it.

Then came the Genie in the Bottle, Paper Money. "Let me out," said the Genie to John Law, the French Banker, "and we'll print money and you'll be the richest man in France!" (This was around 1717.) They did. It worked: then bust the government.

"Let me out," said the Genie to George Washington, "and I'll print United States Continental Dollars and pay for the whole war." "Ask John Adams," said George Washington. They did it. The Continental Dollars flew to the sky; nobody lost except honest, patriotic people who sold their land and houses for them to help the war. The Genie, liberated, went to France. "Let's have a Revolution," he said. "Come on, we'll print Assignats and Mandats." They printed them till their arms were tired—forty-five billion francs. This broke the rich, and impoverished the poor. Those who objected were guillotined.

Europe gasped. "Never again," said the bankers and economists. "Irredeemable paper money," went into the British Litany of the days of John Stuart Mill and Macaulay as "Irredeemable Sin." Never again.

That was all right no doubt—as a Litany, as what we call a counsel of perfection. But the Devil of it was, or rather the Genie of it was, that the first stages of inflation were always so pleasant, so easy, so stimulating—high wages for everybody, jobs for all, and you pay for it all with a printing press! Brandy was nothing beside it as a pick-me-up.

So the Genie could always break loose again, whenever a war gave him a start, a Civil War with a Confederate spiral and a Greenback spiral and later, the great spiral which encircled all Europe, dragging it down to its later doom—an octopus hidden in the Waters of Peace.

Then the Genie of the Bottle joined hands with other devils worse than himself. For he was just an economic devil, and they were devils of perverted Nationalism, turned to cruelty and aggression, to make this present war.

Now what happens? Paper money, and bank credits and checks are all the same thing: all reflect the increasing mechanism of purchase that is bound to shoot up prices if goods run short and people scramble for them. Hence each increase of paper wages means more and more buyers for the same quantity of goods or even for a less quantity as available labour falls. It looks inevitable, doesn't it? . . . And then if prices go up, wages and salaries must go up after them to let people have, as seems only fair, the same goods as they had before. That's what happened in the last war. Prices rose from one to three, even in countries (United States, Britain, Canada) where the currency didn't blow up: in France about five to one.

But the trouble was they didn't fight inflation from the right end. If you attack inflation only by trying to fix prices by law, it blows up as certainly as high explosive will explode: the more you confine it the bigger the burst. When you check prices, you must also check consumption—less and less for everybody—eat what there is and then go without. The old war-time high prices meant a scramble to pay more and more for each article. The rich got it: the poor lost out.

Hence the wizards are now handling the high voltage by refusing to let the current leap into the heap of goods, driving the lions from cage to cage and not letting them taste blood. In plain language, inflation can be beaten out by drastic control of consumption—leaving the people with nothing to buy. Carrying it to an extreme of argument, this "consumption check" against inflation could conceivably go on till the last man died of starvation—in his oldest clothes.

Hence much of our seeming inflation, our first slips into danger, are really illusory. The man with the paper wages has nothing to buy. "Look at that, and that!" he says, as a miser idiot shows dead leaves as his money.

It gets deep, doesn't it? Can we hang on—in the United States, in Canada, in Britain, holding down prices and holding down wages, as best we may? Can we hold it! It's like holding back a team with a heavy-loaded wagon on a steep hill—hard, but it *can* be done—I've seen good teamsters do it —but let the team lose their footing for one moment, and it's all over.

That's the hill we're going down now—steady! steady! But don't be afraid.

V

AMONG HIS MANY ACHIEVEMENTS, STEPHEN LEACOCK
HAD GAINED THE POSITION OF UNOFFICIAL AMBASSADOR
OF GOOD WILL BETWEEN THE UNITED STATES AND
CANADA. IN HIS OWN WORDS, IN THE PREFACE TO "ALL
RIGHT, MR. ROOSEVELT," HE PLEADS AS HIS RIGHT TO
SPEAK HIS "THIRTY-FIVE YEARS ON THE STAFF OF
MC GILL UNIVERSITY OF WHICH HE IS NOW A PRO-
FESSOR EMERITUS; HIS YEARS AS A STUDENT AT THE
UNIVERSITY OF CHICAGO, FROM WHICH HE HOLDS
A DOCTOR'S DEGREE; HIS HONORARY DEGREES FROM
BOSTON AND DARTMOUTH UNIVERSITIES; THE INDUL-
GENT RECEPTION BY THE AMERICAN PUBLIC OF THE
FIFTY VOLUMES HE HAS WRITTEN; AND THE ACQUAINT-
ANCESHIP HE HAS BEEN PRIVILEGED TO MAKE IN
TWENTY YEARS OF PUBLIC LECTURING BEFORE AMERI-
CAN COLLEGES AND AMERICAN AUDIENCES."

Uncle Sam, Good Neighbour

An Allegory

I wonder how the United States came to be the United States? I mean, how it came to take on its peculiar national character, as a sort of "neighbour" to all the world. As the years and the decades, and now even the centuries have gone past, we can begin to see this peculiar aspect of the United States, unknown anywhere else in history.

It is not imperial dominion, in fact it's not dominion or domination at all, but just a peculiar result of mingled merit, destiny and good fortune. People all over the world—Chinese in Chow Chow and Patagonians in Pat Pat—"look to the United States," as a sort of neighbour to appeal to, and to borrow from, just as among the earlier settlers in this country.

Ah! That's it! I see it now—the early settlers. That's where they got it from.

I think there must have been, I mean way back in early settlement times, a country store at a crossroads—you know the kind of place. I mean, store and post office and a farm combined, and this one called Sam's place. And the man who kept it they came to call Uncle Sam. They called him that when he was a long, slouching young man, and then when he was a long, slouching middle-aged man, and finally as a long, slouching old man—old or oldish—I don't think he ever really looked old. But they always called him Uncle Sam.

There were always one or two loafers in the store, sitting on nail kegs and whittling sticks. Uncle Sam sold pretty well everything, but, as a matter of fact, the neighbours seemed to do far more borrowing than buying.

In would come a little girl. "Please, Mr. Sam, ma would like the loan of one of your teakettles."

"Now, which are you?" says Uncle Sam. "You're little Nicaragua, aren't you? Well, tell your ma she hasn't sent back that iron pot yet."

Or they came and bought things and just "charged" them.

In flounces a big, dark girl, all colour and style.

"Uncle Sam," she says, "let me have another yard of that red calico."

Uncle Sam takes his scissors.

"Are you paying for it, Miss Mexico?"

"No, charging it."

"Well, I suppose you've got to have it, and tell your pa that I paid him for the coal oil and he hasn't delivered it yet."

Yet Uncle Sam prospered—oh, ever so much! You see, the farm was a wonderful bit of land, and he owned a tannery and a sawmill—oh, he had everything! Money just seemed to come without trying. "It is a good location," he said.

So, of course, all the neighbours seemed poor as beside Uncle Sam, and it was just natural that they borrowed his things and charged things and didn't pay, and ate candy ("conversation lozenges") out of the open barrel. He took it easily enough. They were, after all, his neighbours. He treated them all the same way; except that there was one spcial lot that used to come now and again, who were evidently favourites. These were settled up North and would come down in summer. "They're folk of my own," says Uncle Sam, "they settled back North but mebbe they'll come home again some day."

To this good neighbourship there was just, perhaps, one exception—or at least not exactly an exception—call it a special case. The reference, of course, is to old Squire Bull, who lived on a fine, big place at quite a little distance, because it was separated from Uncle Sam's corners by the whole extent of a big millpond, so big it was like a lake. From Sam's place you could just see the tops of Squire Bull's grand house and stables.

John Bull was his name, and he liked to call himself "plain John Bull," but all the neighbours knew that was just nonsense, for everybody saw that he was "stuck up" and couldn't be "plain" if he tried. Uncle Sam just couldn't get on to him; and that was a funny thing because they were cousins, their folks having originally come from the same part of the country. Sam always used to deny this—at least when he was young. "He's no cousin of mine," he said. Later, as he got older, he said, "Mebbe he is," and later still, "Oh, I shouldn't wonder." But he said it grudgingly.

For one thing Squire Bull irritated Uncle Sam by always referring to him as if he were just a boy—"that young man," or "young Sam," and yet here they were both old men, or getting close to it. And Squire Bull didn't like to admit that, in point of money and consideration and standing, Uncle Sam was just as good as he was.

That's the way they lived, anyway, till a reconciliation came about in the queerest way. It happened there came a gang of bandits to the settlement, or at any rate, the rumour of them. They were reported as robbing here and plundering there. People began to lock up the doors at night—a thing never done before—and you couldn't be sure of travelling the roads in safety. Quite a few had been robbed, and one or two killed.

Some people wanted to organize and get together and hunt the bandits down. But Squire Bull wouldn't believe in the stories about bandits. "All nonsense," he said, "and if any of the fellows come around my place they'll get a dose of cold lead."

Uncle Sam didn't do anything either. He was a peaceable fellow, never liking to interfere. "Keep out of quarrels" was his maxim. Yet he had a musket and a powder horn hanging in the store, and they said that when it came to shooting he was the best shot in the section. He never talked of it, but really he had been in the Indian War as a young man.

Well, one day, late in the afternoon, toward dusk, some of the children came rushing breathless into the store. "Mr. Sam, Mr. Sam!" they called. "Mr. Sam, the bandits have come, the gang of bandits; they're over at Squire Bull's place."

"What's that? What's that?" said Uncle Sam, all confused.

"The bandits, they're over at Squire Bull's. We saw them smashing in the gates of the yard. We heard the shots. Oh, Mr. Sam, will they kill Mr. Bull?"

"Eh, what?" says Uncle Sam. "Smashing in the gates?"—he seemed hesitating—"hold on! What's that? By gosh, that's gunshots. I heard them plain."

In ran another child, wide-eyed with fright.

"Mr. Sam, come quick, they're over at Mr. Bull's and they've shot some of the help!"

"Is Squire Bull killed?"

"No, he ain't killed. He's in the yard with his back to the wall . . . his head's all cut . . . but he's fighting back something awful."

"He is, is he?" said Uncle Sam, and now he didn't hesitate at all. "Hand me down that powder horn, sis." He took the musket off the wall, and he took out of a drawer a six-shooter derringer that no one knew he had.

The children watched him stride away across the field faster than another man would run. Presently they heard shouting and more shots, and then there was silence.

It was just about dark when Uncle Sam came back, grim and dusty, his hands blackened with powder. The children stood around while he was hanging up his musket and his powder horn.

"Did you get the thieves?" they ventured timidly.

"The gol-darned scoundrels," the old man muttered, "there's some of them won't steal again, and the rest will be safe in jail for years to come. Too bad," he added, "some of them came of decent folks, too."

"And how's Squire Bull, is he killed?" the frightened children asked.

"Killed? No, sir!" laughed Uncle Sam, "he's too tough a piece of hickory for that. His head's tied up in vinegar but he's all right. We had a good laugh over it. He allowed I needn't have come, but I allowed I won the whole fight. We had quite an argument. But here, don't you get in my way, children. Hand me that clothesbrush and reach me down that blue coat off the peg, the one with the long tail—now, that hat."

"But you ain't never going out again, Mr. Sam, are you?"

"Sure, I am. I'm going back over to Squire Bull's. He's giving a party. Now hand me down those cans off that shelf."

And with that Uncle Sam began pulling canned salmon and canned peaches off the store shelves. "I thought I'd bring 'em along," he said. "That darned old fool—why didn't he say he was getting hard up? I don't believe the folks in his house have been fed right for months. . . . Pride, I suppose! . . . Still he's a fine man, is Squire Bull. My own cousin, you know, children."

All Right, Mr. Roosevelt

(*Canada and the United States*)

IT's all right, Mr. Roosevelt, about this business of arms and embargo and the shipment of war material to us over here in Canada. I mean, if you can send us over a lot of first-class machine guns, that's fine! We know just where to use them. But if not, send us some shotguns. They'll do. And if you can't, perhaps you could ship us over some of those old muskets that we used against one another in the battle of New Orleans, and that have been hanging up on the wall for over a hundred years of peace. Send us them. But if you can't, that's all right, because all these Canadian boys are going over to the war, anyway, even if they have nothing to shoot with but Fly-Tox.

But if you can't send anything, it's all right! Don't let that or anything else interfere for a moment with the wonderful association in friendship that has grown up between our country and yours. Let's keep that, anyway. Whatever happens, don't let this continent go the way of Central Europe: let nothing and nobody betray us into that. I am sure you grasp just what I mean. Don't let us let—no, that's a poor phrase— I mean, let no one let—that is to say, it's taken a hundred years of good will to place our northern continent where it stands, and we mean to keep it there.

I remember a while ago hearing my friend Bob Benchley, speaking at a Canadian-American luncheon in New York, ask where else in the world could you find another case like ours— three thousand miles of forts and not a single frontier? And none of us could think of any. Somebody suggested China and Japan. But it doesn't seem the same.

It took a hundred years, more than that, a century and a quarter, to make that frontier as it is—with long care and effort, most of it unconscious and working by an instinct of good will, and without a plan till it was laid down, till the rugged wilderness of nature and of animosity that once separated us was laid down as flat and even as a bowling green.

A bowling green—that reminds me! I remember, years ago up in my part of the country, an old fellow who kept a summer hotel and laid down a bowling green for his guests in front of it. And he had it rolled, beautifully rolled down into such gentle slopes and inclines, with little hollows that you couldn't see, that the bowls would go rolling exactly to the right spot, mistakes corrected themselves, and every one found himself a fine player. And the old man would stand and watch the opponents play and would call to one of them, "Well done!" and then, "Well done!" to the other, and then, "Well done, both of yous!" . . . Well, that's our frontier, and on it and across it we carry on our friendly and unending game. Don't let's spoil it. You can't get turf like that in a day.

So it's all right, Mr. Roosevelt. For, you see, we are not asking anything—we have never taken our relations with you in that way. If we had, we'd long since have been a mere puppet, a shadow. But we are not Manchukuo! No, sir. . . . Just where it is I don't know, but we're not it anyway, and it sounds just the kind of thing not to be.

You see, we have never taken the Monroe Doctrine that way—it never meant to us that in case of danger we were to throw our arms around your neck and shout, "Save us!" No, sir, don't be afraid: there isn't a farmer in Alberta or a lumberman in the shanties who will throw himself around your neck . . . Perhaps the girls may later on, if you're good, but that's different.

And it's all right, too, about the other aspects of the situation; I mean, things like the enlistment of soldiers from your country into ours. . . . If any of the boys are coming over to enlist, and you allow it, there's a welcome and a place for any of them. If any of the McGruders of Mississippi—they were Highlanders, weren't they originally?—want to come over and join the Royal Highlanders in Toronto, we've a tartan and sporran and a jorum (one forgets these Highland terms) for each of them. Let them all come. Perhaps they can bring the Virginia Robinsons and Randolphs with them, or "round-heads" from Connecticut, still stamped with the image of the Ironsides, or the Lowells or the Cabots from Boston—but no, I forgot, they don't talk to anybody—or to nobody that they'd meet in Europe. But if the boys can't come, it's too bad, but we'll understand it. They would if they could, and if not, let them string out along the border and sit and listen to the skirl of the bagpipes and the march of the battalions, all in threes, as the new army of our Dominion goes by.

The marching feet—tramp! tramp! tramp!—in every city of Canada, and soon in every village and hamlet and on every roadside—the tramp, tramp of the marching feet of those who go to war. Tramp, tramp, till the sound of it, the beat of it, stamps into the mind of all the rest of us the sense of duty for each and all of us, whether young or old, whether rich or poor, that tells us to do something, if not in arms, then with pick, or pen, or shovel in the cause for which they go.

So, in such a cause, and with such an aim, I want to set down here how this, our unwritten American alliance, came about, and what is the background that enables it to stand as it does. It needs no guarantees or scraps of paper or pacts. We leave pacts to Judas Iscariot who first trafficked in one. Our alliance has no more "axis" than the axles of our lumber wagons. But it holds as deep in the soil as a New England elm. Tear it out with the stump-extractor of evil tongues and angered quarrels, and you can never set it back.

Let us first turn back the pages of our history. You remember your American Revolution, do you not, that ended with the surrender of—well, never mind, that's just a little painful;

say, it ended with the Peace of 1783. And then it turned out, and has been turning out more and more as kindlier eyes looked at it, in the colours of the sunset, that it wasn't a revolution at all. No, sir, nothing of the sort!—just another triumph of British freedom on the soil of America. You see, the quarrel was really a family quarrel, as between cousins, a sort of civil war, with all kinds of people, good and bad, on each side, and ever so many people, the wiser people, on both sides. Because when a war is unjust and brutal and evil, the wise man takes a side in it once and for all and never leaves it. But in a friendly family quarrel like the American Revolution, the wise man is prepared to say, "Well done, both of yous!" And so it was.

The British themselves saw it first. They discovered after the Revolution, as I say, that it was a great triumph for British freedom, and that George Washington was a typical English country gentleman. In fact, they annexed the whole thing, made it part of British school history, called it "manifest destiny," and recommended it to all other quieter colonies: just as a mother, don't you know, always likes best the bad boy of the family.

And the Loyalists, the refugees who left the States so as to stay under the old flag? Well, that was queerer still. You see, some of them left because of the old flag and some because of other reasons—in fact they *had* to leave, but we won't talk of it. Anyway, they left and a lot of them went to the Maritime Colonies and the greater bulk of them, perhaps ten thousand, went past the maritime settlements on up the St. Lawrence—their pilgrimage, would you believe it, took the best of a year. They wintered in the snows of Sorel, and in the spring they went on up the river to Lake Ontario. Some of them settled on the river and some all along the lake, and as ever so many of them were from New York State, they had really come back home again. You see, they didn't exactly know where they were going—geography was pretty thin then—and all they knew was that they were striking out to make a home in the wilderness, and it turned out that the wilderness was home.

You remember, Mr. Roosevelt, when you opened up that new Friendship Bridge across the river near Gananoque, and all the girls here went wild about it—1938, wasn't it? Well, that was there—I mean, those were it. Those people on the two sides of the ribbons you cut had been waiting to come across and hug one another again for a hundred and fifty years.

Now a strange thing was that those Loyalists who had come from New York, all the way around the St. Lawrence, were joined by another group of Loyalists who came across where your bridge is. These were all Highlanders, settled in the back-woods of New York Province, and formed during the war into the King's Royal New York Regiment. When the war was over, they were disbanded and moved with their families to Upper Canada, alongside the river, and a year later five hundred more Highlanders came out from Glengarry, and presently a thousand more. Thus rose our Scottish Settlement of Glengarry; partly from your people and partly from the homeland. For a full hundred years they still spoke, and preached, in the Gaelic. And of their descendants, some of them, as I write these lines, are close beside me here, at drill on the campus of McGill University as a part of the Highland Regiment, the Black Watch of Canada. Their drill floods all the campus with the moving lines of colour of the khaki and the tartans. And in the pauses of their drill, they sit in little groups upon the grass, like children in a daisy chain, to listen to a sunburned sergeant read from a manual of Active Service in War.

But I turn back to our history. When all those people, and those who followed in their footsteps in the next few years, got settled in Upper Canada, though they called themselves "Loyalists," they were nonetheless Americans. They brought with them from New England their Thanksgiving Day Turkey and from New York the "York Shilling" that was our count of money there till yesterday, or at least till I myself remember it there sixty years ago. And we had, too, the "little red schoolhouse" framed on the Massachusetts model in a school "section." I was a "scholar" in one myself. Notice that —a "scholar": who ever heard in England such a use of the word? It's ours and yours exclusively. In the "little red schoolhouse" we learned out of the same spellers and readers, practically, as you did: we recited with you William Cullen Bryant's *Prairies* and Longfellow's *Excelsior*, and wondered, just as you did, where the uncomfortable boy was trying to climb to.

The other loyalists, I say, stayed in the Maritime Provinces and made a new one, New Brunswick, all for themselves. But instead of becoming angry enemies to your Republic, they turned into a sort of outlying part of New England, with Harvard University as the capital of the Maritime Provinces, the Mecca of all its student pilgrims. Thither, when the Maritimes got started in their great export industries—fish and brains—went all the gifted students of the provinces. It is only of late years that with great difficulty we've been able to coax them away. Even now they're apt to slip off to Harvard, as boys run away to sea, and later, like the runaway boys, turn up as notable men, college presidents and doctors and divines. They're strong on divinity. You have to be in a country as bleak as the Nova Scotia coast.

So that was how our history started and that was the way it kept going on. Quarrels that refused to turn to hate, animosities that broke down into friendship, seeds of dissension sown in a soil that brought them up again as flowers. Such is our history. Are we going to falsify it now?

Let the vanishing feet pass on, and let the armies go, weaponed or weaponless, so that your hearts go with them— that is all we ask, or that at least is the chief thing we ask. . . . But, by the way, I suppose you couldn't lend us— you haven't got a loose dime, have you, Mr. Roosevelt?—but we'll come to that presently. And if you haven't, it's all right.

England will give it to us, and then we'll lend it back again, do you see, like a little boy buying a present for mother.

So, as I say, our history was like that all along. There was the war of 1812. We can't get it quite straight now, what it was all about, but it makes great "pictures." Did you see the one with the White House in it? But what that war was *for*, we can no more make out now than old Caspar could with his. It was something to do with "pressing" sailors, but it's all gone now, "pressed and cleaned" like the rest of our history, as fragrant as old lavender in a cedar chest. As a matter of fact, as in all our conflicts and quarrels, both kinds of people seem to have been on both sides. Why, in the Upper Canada of that day, of its 80,000 inhabitants, only 35,000 represented the Loyalists and their children, and 25,000 were "American" settlers who had come in on their own account, and the rest (20,000) had wandered in from the old country. And, per contra, ever so many Americans thought the declaration of war was a policy of madness, and the Governor of Massachusetts issued a proclamation (June 26, 1812) for a public fast for a wrong committed "against the nation from which we are descended and which for many generations has been the bulwark of the religion we possess."

Or take your Civil War! My, didn't we spring to your help! Yes, sir! on both sides! We fought in the Northern armies, lent money to the South, took in refugees—they annexed our towns of Cobourg and Old Niagara and have never left—we supplied hay and oats at a bare cost (or pretty bare: farmers will be farmers) and when it was over we exulted with the North, shed tears with the South, and have glorified Lincoln and the Union along with you ever since.

Then you remember—at least I can, ever so well—the Venezuela boundary dispute about the Essoquibo River that broke into sudden tumult round Christmas of 1895. England very nearly called out the Household Troops (out of the bars), and you almost mobilized the Texas Rangers, only they were moving too fast. And in six months it was all over, and nobody could remember where the Essoquibo River was and they hadn't known anyway, and the Household Troops went in again for another beer, and the Texas Rangers went on ranging.

So have all our emergencies and quarrels and animosities passed and gone overhead like April showers, or summer thunder, only to clear the air.

You see the underlying reason of all this is the queer inter-mingling of our history and our population. Those loyalists were only just the beginning of it. All through a century and a half our populations have washed back and forward over the line. Why, if at the present moment you count up all the people born in Canada and still alive, fourteen out of every hundred are living in the United States, a total of 1,250,000 in all. And conversely, 350,000 American-born people are living among us. Our Dominion Statistician told your American Statistical Society the other day, when they made him President of it—(we get jobs like that all the time)—he told them that of the people "of Canadian stock," one-third are living in the United States.

Sometimes the tide rises into a flood in one direction, and then turns to an ebb in the other. Back in the eighties, when the mortgages fluttered down on our farms like snowflakes, there was so great a wave that for every 1,000 added to the native born of Canada, there were 726 outgoing emigrants to the United States: not the same individuals, but the same proportion. That was largely the great exodus of the French Canadians moving into New England so steadily and in so large a volume that the Pelletiers and the Dufresnes began to outnumber the Smiths and the McLeans. About 150,000 French Canadians moved across the line between 1875 and 1890, by which date there were 395,000 people in the United States who were French Canadian born, and of these 275,000 in New England. In spite of "repatriation," the French Canadians, by birth or descent, in the United States now number about—I forget what.

But a few years later, to even up the balance, there came your American invasion of our Northwest. When the farmers of the Kansas prairies saw their farms blowing away north-westward in clouds of dust, they followed after their farms and landed in Alberta. They came in caravans of prairie schooners, or by the new railways, with carload lots of furniture, children and household goods—people of substance moving into the promised land, as the Israelites had moved, or the overland immigrants in the prairie schooners moving on California. Before this exodus, only about 500 Americans a year had come into our Northwest, but in 1900 there came 15,000; in 1911, 100,000, and 139,000 in the banner year of 1913; in all 600,000. Our official calculation was that the immigrants, at the height of the exodus, brought in money and goods and property to the value of $1,000 per person.

All this interchange of population, one might think, would have to lead to amalgamation, to the "annexation" of Canada by the United States, or of the United States by Canada. "Annexation," indeed, used to be the bogey of our Canadian politics, the turnip on a stick with a candle in its mouth, used to frighten the electors. It is a dead topic now. It seemed odd the other day to read in the papers that one of our most patriotic statesmen, speaking in Toronto, made a passionate appeal for us not only to get into the war but to get into it good and hard, for fear we might be invaded by Nazis and then the United States would have to drive them out and, as a result, we'd get annexed to the United States. Funny kind of argument, wasn't it! But, you see, way back in the past, there was a time when many of our leading statesmen, in England and over here, were always afraid of Canada's getting too friendly with the United States, just as on a respectable farm they don't like their daughters' going around too much with the hired man. You can't tell what may happen. Well, that was us.

Annexation to the United States! What a strange part that idea, that phrase, has played in our history and how completely it has passed out of it. It has served as a sort of bogey or warning—just as children are told that the Devil will get them if they're not good—or as an invitation out of darkness into light, out of tyranny into freedom, as when Benjamin Franklin came up to Montreal in 1775, expecting to draw down the Canadians as easily as he drew down lightning. But the Canadians, pretty well all French then, weren't taking any. The United States, or rather, the American Colonies, seemed far too British, too protestant, for their taste. So annexation slept. But in the war of 1812 it was the other way. So many Upper Canadians by that time sympathized with the United States and wanted to join the republic that it has been estimated (see our Canadian Archives, Q. 107, p. 236, or else take my word for it) that one-third of the population was on the American side. But as at least one-half of the New England people were on the British side, that only evens things up. That's the queer way our history's been conducted all through—both sides on each side. By which means they were able to keep the war of 1812 going till they got word from Europe that it was over. Luckily they had time, while the news was still on the ocean, to fight the battle of New Orleans which gave us that moving picture that I mentioned.

So annexation slept again. In any case, it didn't matter much whether it slept or woke during the next generation (1815-45), because by that time the people were migrating out of the British Isles in all directions, with ever so many places to go to and all good—with a choice of the old flag or a new flag or no flag at all—the States, or to British North America or Australia or New Zealand or the Cannibal Isles. The migration to British North America between 1820 and 1845, apart from an odd year of slump, was anything from 10,000 to 66,000; to the States, from 10,000 to 63,000; to the Antipodes (apart from a banner year of 32,000 in 1841), from 1,000 to 15,000. The King of the Cannibal Isles kept no statistics of newcomers. He dealt with them as they came.

Then came (after 1845) the slump caused by free trade, free navigation and free competition, with such a big dose of freedom straight out of Manchester that it was just like the Kingdom of Heaven—to those who had was given and from those who had not was taken even what they had. Canada, half-developed and rickety, went under. "All the prosperity of which Canada is thus robbed"—it is Lord Elgin, the Governor of 1849, who says this, not me—"is transplanted to the other side of the line, as if to make Canadians feel more bitterly how much kinder England is to the children who desert her than to those who remain faithful. The conviction that they would be better off if annexed is almost universal among the commercial classes at present." So there you were! No wonder that the commercial interests, along with a lot of other interests, presently got out at Montreal an Annexation Manifesto (1849) in favour of "friendly and peaceful separation." We used to keep this wicked document hidden away in our archives, but now that it doesn't matter we can admit that it was signed by a prime minister and three cabinet ministers of the later Dominion and with most of the best names in the city. We can laugh it off at that. That's the beauty of our joint history. It all laughs off so easily.

But the Manifesto didn't matter, because the wind turned around and blew the other way. There came the Reciprocity Treaty of 1854 and the Crimean War and wheat at $2.50 a a bushel, and then your Civil War, with hay and hogs for everybody to sell till the Upper Canada farmers got so rich that they built brick houses and frame barns (in place of logs), and then put mortgages on them and built more of them—bigger and brighter—till they got so far into debt that they have never got out of it; in fact, so far into debt that they had to put on more mortgages still. That's the way with farmers. In a burst of prosperity, they put on mortgages—that's called expansion—and when debt comes they put on more, which is called contraction. The two together make the economics of large farming as opposed to small, or subsistence, farming. In the latter, subsistence farming, you just live; in the big stuff, you just don't. But, of course, there's no need to tell Americans about that. It's been part of your economic history as much as ours: only being a bigger country you were able to do it on a bigger scale, especially in the west where there's room. I've seen it. In one of the big agricultural states of the Mississippi valley, I have been driven for half an hour over one and the same mortgage. The grand old estates in Scotland have nothing on us. But I only mention it to show the similarity of our history, and the sympathy of it.

Annexation came back in 1891, but it was just a shadow of itself, not much reality to it. We had all got hard up again in Canada with the premature break of the Manitoba Boom, and a lot of our people turned again to Annexation as a sort of old family remedy—just as farmers turn to Painkiller and Bloodbitters for pretty well everything. It was mostly for election use, anyway, but the cry didn't work. So instead of joining the States we did the other thing and let down the bars of the Northwest and advertised for American farmers, and we got the invasion that I spoke of above. . . . And this time we got such a "boom" in the Northwest that the first one, of the early Eighties, sounded like a whisper. While it lasted we had time to bring into the West, as I said, 600,-000 of your people, and build half a dozen big cities and run railroads all over Hades in the prairie grass, ready for cities not built yet. That's the way we do it, like carpenters putting up a grandstand before the rain comes. There is going to be another boom in the Nineteen Forties, and if we work fast we can build a metropolis or two and half a dozen universities while it's still on.

So after that we never really needed to fall back on Annexation any more, and never have—except once, more or less in fun, just to make an election. That was back in 1911, which begins to seem like ancient history now, all peace and sunshine and such a thing as a "World War" just a fanciful dream of the imagination. Elections in days like those had none of the grim reality of life and death in which we live now. They were made up of fifty per cent business and fifty per cent humbug. You had, of course, to start an "issue," and if there was none in sight in a clear sky you had to make one, as an Alberta rainmaker makes rain. So this time the Liberals said to the Conservatives, "How about annexation?" —and the Conservatives said, "First-rate, which side do you want?"—because both sides had had each. It was like the way in which the "scholars" in the little red schoolhouse used to decide on who should have first innings by throwing a baseball bat and matching hands on it. So the Liberals took Annexation and lost out on it.

Looking back on it now after nearly forty years, it all seems coloured with the evening light of retrospect. Nor do I remember any great angers over it at the time. One of our great arguments on the platform (I was a Conservative in that election) was to quote a letter of your good Mr. Taft, the President, in which he had spoken of our becoming an "Annex" of the republic. I think he meant it as a compliment, just as one speaks with pride of the expansion of a hotel. But naturally for us, "Taft's letter" became the target of heroic denunciation. We used to carry it around, copies of it, to election meetings and have it on the speaker's table, beside the water jug, as Exhibit No. 2—right after the telegrams from all the distinguished people who would not be at the meeting—a little touch that lends class to a political gathering. It's not who's there that counts; it's who's not.

Years after we gave a big dinner to Mr. Taft at the University Club in Montreal, when he had long finished being President and was up here as an "arbitrator" to decide whether the Grand Trunk Railway was worth nothing or less than nothing. In introducing Mr. Taft, the Chairman read out from bygone newspapers those old denunciations of Mr. Taft and added, "Look at him! The man has the face of a Mephistopheles!" And Mr. Taft, smothered with laughter, admitted that he had.

So what I mean to say is, that's all that ultimately came of this bogey of Annexation that frightened two generations in their sleep. It ended in a banquet and a laugh. And now all that's left of it is that our local societies along the border annex pieces of the United States; the Rotarians of Buffalo annex St. Catharine's for a day—see the Stars and Stripes all over the place, "Welcome Rotarians!" The Girl Guides of Windsor annex Detroit (Union Jacks everywhere and "Welcome Girl Guides!"). As I write these lines, the American Hotel Men have annexed Montreal in such numbers that we're short of flags. Indeed, if any one wants to understand our relations with one another better than history can tell or statistics teach, let him go and stand anywhere along the Niagara-Buffalo frontier at holiday time—fourth of July or first of July, either one—they're all one to us. Here are the Stars and Stripes and the Union Jacks all mixed up together and the tourists pouring back and forward over the International Bridge; immigration men trying in vain to sort them out; Niagara mingling its American and Canadian waters and its honeymoon couples. . . . Or go to the Detroit-Windsor frontier and move back and forward with the flood of commuters, of Americans sampling ale in Windsor and Canadians sampling lager in Detroit . . . or come here to Montreal and meet the Dartmouth boys playing hockey against McGill . . . or if that sounds too cold, come to Lake Memphremagog in July and go out bass fishing and hook up the International Boundary itself.

But all of such fraternization is only all the more fraternal because we know that we are satisfied on each side of the line to keep our political systems different. Annexation in the old bygone sense has vanished out of the picture. And in the other sense of a union of friendship that needs neither constitution nor compacts, we have it now and mean to keep it. Just once indeed—last spring, you remember—it looked almost the other way around, when we nearly annexed your republic; in fact, we *did* annex it (and you with it, Mr. Roosevelt) for three days during the visit of the King and Queen. I believe we had to remind you that we saw them first and wanted them back.

What a wonderful visit it is to look back upon now, like a break of open sky and sunshine in the gathering clouds. Up and down through Canada we dragged the King and the Queen by the hand, like children anxious to show our treasures—the apple blossoms of Annapolis and the peach-bloom of Niagara and the flowers among the ripening wheat of the prairies. "Take this, and this, and this," in handfuls and, "if ever England wants anything—." And now England has sent over, not for the flowers of the gardens or the plains, but for the hard metal, nickel and copper and steel, from the rocks of our northern desolation. These are the grim blossoms that go out as the harvest from Canada, gathered for its army. Under the tramp of the marching feet of those that carry it, our ears can catch the undertone of music—like the subdued refrains of the theatres, half-heard, half-lost in the other sounds—can catch the refrain of fifty years ago:

> "for they're sol-diers of the Queen, my lads—
> the Queen—my lads . . ."

till it fades and dies on the ear as the footsteps pass into distance.

I spoke of migration. But the shift of population back and forward that binds us most has not meant the mass movement of any special exodus or influx, but the steady and continued outgoing of individuals, seeking their fortunes back and forward across the line. From this has grown the unity of our professions—the law that follows the English common law in forty-seven states and in eight provinces—with two honourable exceptions to remind us of the bygone claims of France; the profession of medicine that sends its students and its professors and its practitioners indifferently across a continent; the engineers, the teachers, the artists, the architects. No one has ever counted, no statistics have ever shown, the volume of this export of brains across the line: or measured up the "unfavourable balance" of any community that dares trade in this with Nova Scotia. But the common experience of those of us whose lot it has been to come and go across the line among the colleges can bear witness to what an incalculable influence it must have had. I speak here of what I know. I "migrated" to the United States, to Chicago, forty years ago, as a wave all by myself, so penurious and friendless that even the thugs wouldn't murder me. Of such single threads, insignificant in themselves, has our common garment been woven.

To the student, who represents the export of brains, we add the tourist, who represents the import of wonder. The habit of leaving home is one of the latest phases of our rapid civilization—as the wheel spins, people fly off from the centrifugal force of it. Arizona marvels at Alberta; Alberta at Arizona. The sound psychological principle of "tourism" is that anywhere is better than home, and if you don't buy a car you can't go anywhere and if you do buy a car you must go somewhere. From which springs the enormous economic phenomenon of "tourism" as a part of international trade. Our latest figures show that American visitors crossing the frontier spend in our country nearly $300,000,000 a year, and our return visitors spend about $100,000,000 a year in the States. Who wins out on this, only Professor Quiz of the Radio could tell, but at least it means that friendly little signs of "tourists," "cabins," and "fresh eggs" voice a welcome from every highway. Even in some lost corner in the broken bush where there is but a falling barn, a tumbled house, and a melancholy, a pathetic handmade sign, there passes to the whispering corn that rustles in the corn patch the word of hope, "tourists." Better this, than the "keep out," "keep off," "military zone" of Europe. Our "demarcation" where the forests still front civilization has as its Siegfried Line the sign, "Fresh Eggs."

That brings me easily enough to talk, as I said above I wished to, about money—you remember—about that dime? After all, you know, in your country as in ours money talks: and when it doesn't talk it whispers. So when I ask you about letting us have that loose dime, I am sure you won't think—that is, that you would fully understand—well, let the dime talk.

What I mean is this. In a sense, we don't need any material aid. The war is going to make our fortune. It is an ill wind that blows no one luck, and the storms of death and disaster let loose to blow over Europe will cast up on our shores as a part of their wreckage a golden harvest of opportunity, a marvellous development of our latent resources. Thus have the sorrows and disasters of Europe always brought fortune to America. Bygone tyranny sent you the Pilgrim Fathers. Scotland sent you its Highlanders after the Forty-Five. Famine in Ireland gave New York its police force, and hard times in Scandinavia redeemed themselves in Minnesota. Even Germany weeded out for you its best, its refugee Karl Schurzes and its Joseph Pulitzers. Every European cycle of hard times, famine or depression, has washed its waves of newcomers to our plains and forests, and raised up in our sunshine a newer generation of hope that would have faded in the European shadow.

Now shall come the greatest of all, the vast migration out of Europe when this war, as yet unnamed, shall end. And this is ours first of all, this is Canada's. We can and will take in half a million British a year, and still feel our country empty for a generation yet. French, too, if they will come: but scarcely likely: once back on the leafy boulevards with a *vin rouge* and a fifth edition of an evening paper, they stay there till the next war. They ask no other consummation than just to get back to their *consommation*.

But the British! Once the example was made of evacuating the children out of London the pace was set. Children who started life by "evacuating" will migrate all over the Empire.

What's the Atlantic to a family that has been all the way to Devon?

But long before the tide, comes the ground swell: and that will be in the call for our resources—men and material, matter and metal, to pass over for our defence on the European front. This, in spite of taxes, in spite of disruptions and dislocations, in spite of the inevitable but brief post-war slump, will make the material future of our country, as the Napoleonic War made yours. We can't help it. We're going to be just as modest about it as we can. But it's there. And, of course, if you people like to come in on it, why, there's lots for all of us. But if not, it's all right anyway.

Take first our gold. From being nothing and nobody in the gold business fifty years ago, we are now the world's second in it, and if you count in the other stuff that comes out with the gold, we are the world's first. Just before the Great War (1911), the world had a total gold stock in hand of about $10,000,000,000 (meaning by a dollar, the twentieth part of an ounce) and a yearly production of $462,000,000. Canada only produced $9,000,000 and only held a negligible stock in its banks for glory's sake. It coined no gold. Most people living in Canada never saw a gold coin. There had been the British Columbia mines and then the Klondike (1898), but their glory passed. Then came the discovery of gold all round Hudson's Bay—God's desolation that shore had seemed—and changed all the face of our country. By the close of the Great War (1919), Canada produced $15,-000,000 of a world's output of $350,000,000; and just before the fall of the gold standard altered the calculation from hard money to soft paper (1931), Canada produced $58,000,-000 of a world's total of $460,000,000. Now, reckoning the ounce of gold at 35 paper dollars, Canada in the last fully reported year produced $165,000,000 worth of gold.

So that's our interest in gold: and as our government buys all the output of the Canadian mines in terms of U. S. paper, the fall of our currency—now at 10 per cent discount—doesn't affect this part of the economic problem. . . .

Now every time that war comes back to the world, gold comes back to its own. When the war is over, the economists begin to explain, as regularly as a chorus at sunset, that the world doesn't need gold. They say that everything that gold does for commerce could be done without it; that as a measure of value you can hardly rely on it from one century to another. At the time of the Norman Conquest, a dollar and a half in gold would buy a cow! Where is that cow now? When King Richard III (not mechanized) shouted, "A horse! a horse! my kingdom for a horse!" he could have had a good one for five dollars. And now his kingdom is mortgaged for forty billions, and carries it easily. . . . That sort of economics worries the business world about as much as the astronomers do when they tell us that the sun is losing time —half a second every thousand years—and that the North Pole star has shifted twenty minutes (or is it seconds?) since the Egyptians looked at it. The economists told us after the last war that gold was as "antiquated as the stagecoach," that instead of it we could use "index numbers" and "ratios" and "curves of demand and supply." But with war, back comes gold as the only means of payment for people too ignorant or stubborn to accept a couple of curves in return for army mules or crude oil. A Turk won't take an Index Number and will look a gift ratio in the mouth.

So when gold comes back, all the warring nations want it and must have it, and all the nations that have mines must make the best of them. If one price (in the paper dollars of the minute) won't get the gold out of the mines, then the price in paper dollars has got to go up. The thing is as logical as a hydraulic pump. In the old days of free coinage, the pump worked of itself: you dug up a dollar ($20.67 per oz.) and you got a dollar, a stamped one with a milled edge, but really just what you dug up. But it comes to much the same thing now: if there's need enough for gold, the paper price has got to go up till the gold is forthcoming.

But here is the oddness of it. Economically, gold is in reverse gear. In hard times, with low wages and low cost for materials and powers, gold beats out its momentary paper price, and mining flourishes best when everything else flourishes worst. This at first sight looks like "Public Enemy No. 1," but it isn't. In fact, it's more likely the other way; it acts like the big flywheel in a machine that helps it to run when the running is hard, and helps slack it up when it needs it. "Compensatory action" is the engineer's phrase, isn't it? If not, they can have it.

So, inevitably, the first effect of war is to raise all prices of labour and materials and machinery, and for the moment knock the profit out of mining. Indeed the very anticipation of this is enough to knock down the stock exchange valuation of the mining shares, as it has done right now. But you can no more hold them down for good than you can sit on a safety valve. The gold is needed, the paper price rises, and up they come! This is happening right now, as easy to predict as sunshine in California. Any one who wants to can make a lot of money out of it. Only be sure to pick the right mines. There are three kinds in Canada—established mines, prospective mines and flapdoodle. The established mines are the ones that are actually producing gold, lots of it, with lots more in sight (that means, technically, gold that you don't see) and in some of them gold is piled up, as in the Egyptian pyramids of the Rameses family, so much of it that the directors can hand down a dividend off the shelf as they hand down raisins in a country store, unless they fall asleep and forget to.

By the prospective mines, I mean the ones that later are going to be, or were going to be, but for the war, established mines. The gold is there for certain, and, apart from changes of transport and conditions and taxes and charges, prospective mines would have turned into established mines as properly as seeds turn into pumpkins. But war changes a lot of things. . . .

The flapdoodle mines outnumber the others, as the blacks outnumber the whites in Barbados. Some of them are just a few stakes in the ground, or a claim, or a hole, or a hope, or a false alarm. Some of them, not a doubt of it, would have turned into Eldorados of profit. And on this basis the flapdoodle mines have given us, in peacetime, a cheerful element of chance in a monotonous world, too prim to allow sweepstakes and without enough time to play Italian lotto or French dominoes: a little element of northern adventure in a dull routine of work, with a dime sent out to seek an Eldorado. Here's to them and good-bye! They have sprung up like little flowers in their northern wilderness, but with the hot blast of war they perish, as the flowers do, in their own bush fires. But with peace again, and with the second growth of underbrush rising anew in the burnt forest, the flapdoodle mines, a new crop, will spring to life again, and their life go on as before.

Such is the gold stake in Canada. You Americans might care to come in on it. It's better than sitting around in Oklahoma, arguing on neutrality. But if not, that's all right; you don't mind my talking of it.

But gold is only the minor part of our mineral resources. That same rim of rocks that encircles the desolate shores of the James and Hudson's Bays is one vast treasure house of the world's metals—iron, copper, cobalt, nickel, lead—and metals whose strange names and magic properties are known only to those whose business it is to forge the mechanisms of war. Our nickel represents 80 per cent of the world's supply. Till now 95 per cent of it went into the arts of peace where its matchless property of hardening other metals puts it beyond competition. But in war the God Mars will claim his own.

But since we have started talking about this low business of gold and money and money getting, let us go a little further with it and recall how much our mutual trade means to each of us. The total of it in the last reported year ran to $900,000,000: but, as the Scotch say, never mind about the three cents. In fact, never mind about the figures at all. I may have got them all wrong: when I say millions, perhaps it was billions. I always feel that figures merely clutter up an argument.

But for those who do enjoy figures, please don't add and subtract the columns to get at the "balance of trade" to see who is cheating who. Of all the fool doctrines that have obscured the commercial outlook of mankind and injured peace and good will among the nations, the balance of trade doctrine is the worst. What does it matter who sells and who buys as long as both are satisfied? If I buy a dozen eggs from my grocer, he has, I admit, the balance of trade, but after all I have the eggs. But according to this fool doctrine the grocer has outdone me by thirty-five cents. Over those points statesmen on your side of the line and statesmen on our side of the line have shouted denunciation for generations. We had the "balance" on you during the Civil War period and cheated you out of so much that you had to shut down on trade with us and terminate the Reciprocity Treaty. Just now and for some years past you've been cheating us regularly every year (see the reports) out of about fifty million dollars (or billion): in short, we would be absolutely on the rocks if we hadn't been able to turn around and cheat the British (who, of course, are easy marks) out of still larger amounts. The British, in fact, are such nuts commercially that they've been running an unfavourable balance of trade for nearly a hundred years and have never caught on to it. Don't whisper it to them or they might wake up.

The so-called unfavourable balance may mean glorious things for a nation. When this war ends, if there should ensue, as I am sure there will, a period of development for Canada such as few countries ever saw—a flood of immigration, a mass import of machinery and a vast development of natural resources—then the balance of trade will be utterly and completely unfavourable, year after year, and the more rapid the development the heavier the adverse balance. The infancy of a nation spells an adverse balance, from the efforts made on its behalf: just as human infancy means an adverse balance of care and kisses. And if a nation turns old, so old that its efforts end, and it sits still and lives on its investments abroad—its feet in warm water and its gruel at its side—then that again leaves the adverse balance, for the gruel. Thus in the life of trade as in the life of man, do youth and age contrast, and age presents its sorry parody of a second childhood.

So in this new period, first of our war and then of our rising industrial development and power, let the balance fall so heavy in the scale that it kicks the beam. Such a balance is measured visibly to the eyes by its actuality of carloads of machinery and material, and is reflected from that into terms of money. But the goods are the substance, the money just the moonshine in the water. When you lend us money and we import material, what has happened really is that you have lent us the material; and when we pay you interest, that also, at one remove, takes the form of handing over goods.

So that brings me, Mr. Roosevelt, to that question I asked way up above, whether you have a loose dime? You may have forgotten it, but I've been thinking of it all through. If you haven't got it, why, that's all right. But if you have, what about lending it to us? I needn't talk to you about our credit and how fine it is, because it's wonderful, except of course in Alberta where they've got it a little too much socialized. But you know what they're like in the West—big-hearted—a sort of effect of the big open spaces—well, never mind them: we'll pay their share.

Now if you were to ask me how much, I would say that depends altogether on what you have. We'll take all you've got, but beyond that we don't want to go. And when I say send us over money, I don't mean, of necessity, send it over to buy the kind of bonds in the table I spoke of. We have

a line of common stocks that we are showing this winter that
I think we can absolutely "guarantee," as they say of the
fresh eggs in our Bon Secours Market here. I hate to come
down from the high level of this discussion to the low ground
of political economy, but I know that I don't need to tell
Americans how beautiful is a dividend that is independent of
the currency it's paid in, because if the currency goes down
the dividend goes up. Our money has fallen, as compared
with yours, by ten per cent: as a matter of fact, all currencies
are falling, like snowflakes coming down together, but some
a little faster than the rest. Our snowflakes are wet and heavy
just now with the gathering tears of war and fall a little
bit faster for it; but we like them nonetheless for that: and
soon the gathered warmth of national effort, peace and victory shall float them up in the sunshine. . . .

But no, never mind all that. It's all right, Mr. Roosevelt.
If your people want to help and lend a hand or lend a dime,
why, that's fine! But if they can't, it's all right; we'll manage.
We've known hard years from our pioneer days down, hard
times and mortgages, and the stress of war, and never yet
broken faith for a day. We'll go down deep and deeper into
our pockets till we turn them inside out into emptiness. Who
could fail to do it, with the tramp of the marching feet in
our streets to remind us that there are higher things than
money, and worse things than poverty? It's all right, Mr.
Roosevelt.

So let me get back again from my discussion of money and
commerce to where I started from, the thesis that nothing
that is to happen in Europe must disturb the peace and good
will that prevails in North America. It has been fashioned in
a mould that, once broken, can never be reset.

Those of us who study the past often think of the British
people as the fortunate children of history; free from invasion
for close upon a thousand years; their institutions struck deep
into soil, ancient as the elms and oaks of their countryside:
antiquity preserved in a hundred quaint and venerable forms,

time's chain upon the present; freedom so long established that it has bred a kindly tolerance that knows no cruelty: that merely touches crime upon the shoulder and says, "Come along with me": lends a soap box to a communist to speak from: and fights and dies without hatred, calling its enemy "Fritz." "That was a fine shot," so said the other day a British Navy Captain before going down with his torpedoed ship, and, saying it, added another line to the golden page.

This same happy destiny, on a still larger scale, of an uninvaded land and an undisturbed peace, is offered to us in North America, as seen in the broad view of history, where a generation is but a day. Shaded and vexed as it is by fierce industrial conflict, it still has moved forward toward enduring peace. The light fights against the darkness. Already the twilight of the dawn is touched with the rising sun.

Over Great Britain, for the moment, a dark shadow has fallen. No one who knows the worth of the British people can doubt that it will pass. Such a people cannot die.

But when the shadow passes, they must not look across a clearer ocean to see. that it has fallen over us. They must see that the broad daylight of peace and good will, which came to us in America from the sunrise out of their islands, has been unshadowed and unvexed, and shall so pass to the noonday of a larger future.

VI

THESE TWO ARTICLES WERE INTENDED FOR AN ANTHOL-
OGY OF HUMOUR, NEVER FINISHED, "NOT TO BE
REGARDED AS AN ATTEMPT TO SELECT THE WORLD'S
BEST HUMOUR BUT AS A PURELY PERSONAL DISCUSSION
OF THE THINGS THAT I HAVE READ AND ADMIRED AND
INVITE PEOPLE TO READ AGAIN WITH ME."

Alice Walks in Wonderland

Alice in Wonderland is one of the world's books. The name is so familiar that the world forgets that it is really two books, *Alice's Adventures in Wonderland* and *Through the Looking-Glass and What Alice Found There*. The first was published in 1865 and the second not till 1871, but they generally pass amalgamated as *Alice in Wonderland*. Few people could remember offhand whether or not the Walrus and the Carpenter were in the same book with the Mad Hatter. But no one doubts the unity of the whole. Book One or Two, it is all Wonderland with the same kind of people in it, found nowhere else.

All of it is the work of Lewis Carroll who was in reality the last person to have written it. His real name was the Reverend Charles Lutwidge Dodgson (1832-1898), and he lived a secluded life in Christ Church College, Oxford, as a clerical don and a fellow and tutor in mathematics. Here life passed easily by, term succeeding term, as sheltered as the quadrangles of the colleges, as timeless as the flow of the River Isis. Here lived a bygone world of cloistered, clerical, classical quiet, a world of learning undisturbed, majestic in its prestige, profound in its very ignorance. Here Greek grammar outranked the maker of the Suez Canal. Yet these cloistered, clerical scholars, walking like rooks in their college quad, maintained in religion essentially the beliefs of the Tennessee fundamentalists, and outside of it a complete ignorance of, and often a complete contempt for, at least one-half of the things that constitute the world's knowledge of today. For them chemistry was a stinking business, geology halfway to hell and electricity better left alone.

In this environment Lewis Carroll fitted like a white mouse in a silk box. He lived in sort of half-seclusion with just enough to do not to have nothing to do, wrote a few mathematical disquisitions, and quite a long theological monograph, but chiefly he revelled in the puzzles and acrostics and conceits of language that come down from scholastic days. Biographers exalt his mathematics for sensation's sake. But, in reality, Lewis Carroll's mathematical writings amounted to nothing more than textbook stuff, juggling Euclid Book V into algebra and so on. His chief theological writing is a little treatise on the problem of eternal punishment in Hell by a loving God, which he shows in a rather misty way to be just the kind of thing that a loving God would institute, if it didn't last too long. It might be so—in Wonderland.

The chief and most obvious personal characteristic of the Reverend Charles Dodgson was his extraordinary fondness for little girls; he loved to loll with them in punts, to nestle with them in the grass beneath a tree, and to tell them neverending stories. This is of course so admirable, especially in a young cleric, that those of us made of rougher metal are not allowed to call it "sissy." But I'd like to—the endless pussy-wussy letters to little girls, the endless willingness to have them in to tea, and to take their photographs in the spacious set of rooms which he enjoyed at Christ Church. A little of that sort of thing may be excellent but, as they say in Yiddish-English, too much is enough.

More than that. The Reverend Mr. Dodgson was not only a sissy in college but a sissy outside of it. He thought swearing terrible, and the faintest touch of scoffing at sacred things, even in fun, distressed his sensitive nature. For example, he thought some of the so-called fun of England's new writer, Mr. W. S. Gilbert, most deplorable stuff. Gilbert, celebrated already for his "Bab" Ballads, had now opened out into the glorious fun of the Gilbert and Sullivan comic operas. But it was too glorious for Lewis Carroll to see; it dazzled his eyes, unused to full daylight. He thought it dreadful of Mr.

Gilbert to make fun of curates and the church. There is in one of the earlier operas, forgotten now, the *Sorcerer*, a delightful song, executed by a Bishop who embodies all the plump and decorous prosperity of his happy office, a song detailing his life as a "pale young curate":

> Time was when love and I were well acquainted,
>> Time was when we walked ever hand in hand;
> A saintly youth with worldly thought untainted,
>> None better loved than I in all the land.
> Time was when maidens of the noblest station,
>> Forsaking even military men,
> Would gaze upon me; rapt in adoration—
>> Ah, me, I was a fair young curate then.
>
> Had I a headache? Sighed the maids assembled;
>> Had I a cold? Welled forth the silent tear;
> Did I look pale? Then half the parish trembled;
>> And when I coughed all thought the end was near.
> I had no care—no jealous doubts hung o'er me—
>> For I was loved beyond all other men.
> Fled gilded dukes and belted earls before me—
>> Ah, me, I was a pale young curate then.

Any one who cannot exult in the fun and thrill to the final cadence of that song has neither music nor humour. But it was too much for Lewis Carroll.

"Mr. Gilbert," he wrote in the London magazine *The Theatre*, "seems to have a craze for making bishops and clergymen contemptible. . . . The *Pale Young Curate* is to me simply painful. I seem to see him as he goes home at night, pale and worn with his day's work, perhaps sick with the pestilent atmosphere of a noisome garret, where, at the risk of his life, he has been comforting a dying man—and is your sense of humour, my reader, so keen that you can laugh at that man? Then be consistent . . . laugh also at the pale young soldier as he sinks on the trampled battlefield" . . .

Quite so. But not all pale young curates lived in the slums. A good many of them played croquet and drank tea on the lawn. That's where they met the gilded earls and belted knights who ran away from them. These boys were not to be met in the slums. Lewis Carroll really shows his limitations. He didn't understand that Gilbert was in fun. We may compare the man mentioned in Harry Graham's *Ruthless Rhymes,* who had a high-spirited, mischievous son Augustus who used to push people under buses: *"I will say this about my son, he does enjoy a bit of fun."* Gilbert wasn't thinking of slums and dying paupers who infested curates. He was like Augustus—just enjoying "a bit of fun." One might as well denounce Lewis Carroll's Jabberwock poem as a scene of hideous bloodshed, or feel horrified when the Duchess' baby turned into a pig and she threw it away. How painful for motherhood.

Still worse is Lewis Carroll's denunciation of the terrible swearing in Gilbert's *Pinafore,* where some one actually says, "Damme."

He writes:

I have never seen Mr. Gilbert's clever play *Pinafore* performed by grown-up actors; as played by children one passage in it was to me sad beyond words. It occurs when the Captain utters the oath, "damme," and forthwith a bevy of sweet, innocent-looking little girls sing, with bright, happy looks, the chorus, "He said, 'Damme me.' He said, 'Damme me.'" I cannot find words to convey to the reader the pain I felt in seeing those dear children taught to utter such words to amuse ears grown callous to their ghastly meaning.

A little while ago (September, 1941) one of the few survivors of the Oxford of that day, Mrs. Margaret Woods, distinguished as the daughter of George Granville Bradley, Dean of Westminster (1821-1903), and on her own account as a novelist, wrote an interesting reminiscence of Lewis Carroll in the Oxford of the Seventies.

The most enduringly famous of the Oxford writers of that date was Lewis Carroll, author of *Alice in Wonderland*. His real name was Dodgson and he was a Senior Student, that is, a Fellow of Christ Church, where he lived a secluded life in his college rooms. He had formerly been intimate with the family of Dean Liddell, the Dean of the College, and the story of Alice had been first told to the Liddell children. When the Alice of his tale had grown into a lovely girl, he asked, in old-world fashion, her father's permission to pay his addresses to her. The Dean might reasonably have refused his permission on the ground of the girl's youth and inexperience, and the discrepancy in age between her and their friend. But Dean Liddell, whose manner was always haughty, rebuffed Mr. Dodgson's appeal in so offensive a way that all intercourse between them ceased. It is an awkward situation for a Fellow of a college not to be on speaking terms with his Head. Mr. Dodgson now took up photography but here also he found a snag. He invited a very little girl to be photographed and took her almost unclothed. Her mother shrieked at the impropriety of this. No wonder the sensitive man of genius became propriety-stricken. Hence the unsatisfactoriness of my own contacts with him. When I was fifteen, he expressed a wish to photograph me and invited my mother to bring me to lunch in his rooms. Their lunch time conversation was not amusing and, as manners for schoolgirls then enjoined, I remained silent. The resulting photograph represented a self-conscious young lady sitting bolt upright in her chair, with a forced smile on her face. My only tête-à-tête with him about a year later was still more unfortunate. I met him at Reading Station where I was changing for Oxford. He was seated in a first class carriage and found that I was alone and travelling third class. This horrified him, not quite so unreasonably as we thought, for there were traps set for young girls on journeys, of which my innocent mother was as ignorant as myself. I got into an empty compartment and to my embarrassment Mr. Dodgson left his first class carriage and joined me there. Seating himself at the furthest end to (sic) myself, he put arithmetical puzzles to me during the rest of the journey. My education had been neglected and not being interested in arithmetic I never learned more than was necessary for keeping accounts. Consequently I could not solve one of his conundrums, and he doubtless concluded me to be a stupid girl, for he took no further notice of me.

So one would think that such a secluded, academic, not to say sissified, young man would be the last person to amuse his more robust compatriots and his rough transatlantic cousins for three generations. And so, indeed, he was in his ordinary walk in life. "I knew and greatly valued Charles Dodgson," wrote one of his intimate friends, "in the friendly intercourse of life; but the friend of the fireside and the family dinner table was totally unlike the Lewis Carroll that popular imagination would picture. I may truthfully say that throughout much friendly intercourse with Charles Dodgson, the remembrance of which I value greatly, I never met that exquisite humourist Lewis Carroll."

For here stepped in a peculiar mystery or magic such as occurs in the creation of literature of exception. It was like Charles Dickens groping his way, leading the Pickwick Club by the bridles of their horses and then turning around a corner into the magic world of Dingley Dell and the *White Hart Inn*; such a world as never was, quite untrue to life, but much better, as all our lives ought to be, and hence more true than life itself. It was like Mark Twain, fumbling around with an attempt at a new Tom Sawyer story, the same old pranks grown stale, and then drifting away down the Mississippi on a raft with Huckleberry Finn. So it was with *Alice in Wonderland*. Lewis Carroll, telling random stories to his little girls, made up as he went along, fell down a rabbit hole into a most extraordinary world of odd characters. He didn't make them up. They just seemed to come; and the odd thing is that these impossible characters always seem to be suggesting something else. It all seems as if we had heard it before; as if it meant something that we don't quite apprehend, and yet recognize; something half-caught and yet slipping away, leaving its unsolved suggestion. We keep asking, as the shifting inconsequential scenes and people pass by, What is that? Who is that like? Where have I heard that?

For example, at the Mad Hatter's Tea-Party which we quote below, when the Hatter and the March Hare shake the Dormouse to wake him up and he says, "I heard every word you fellows were saying." . . . Surely we have heard that before. It sounds so familiar—yes!—men together in the evening and one who dozes off from too much open-air exercise—that's exactly what it is!

But Lewis Carroll himself could only guess what the characters meant and where the talk came from. "Bits and scraps," he said, "every idea and nearly every word of the dialogue *came of itself.* . . . I pictured to myself the Queen of Hearts as a sort of embodiment of ungovernable passion . . . the Red Queen a fury, but cold and calm. . . . The White Queen gentle, stupid, fat and pale, and helpless as an infant . . . suggesting imbecility but never quite passing into it." It was a queer process that went on in his brain; something half-suggested, a peculiar power to write half an idea, which the reader half-gets. When he was asked what *The Hunting of the Snark* meant, Lewis Carroll answered truthfully that he didn't know. He said that he was walking one day on a hillside when it suddenly occurred to him that "the Snark was a Boojum." This was like one of the revelations of the Old Testament. More was revealed later—"pieced itself together"—he said. So the Snark remains an unfathomed mystery.

These fancies were first precipitated into written form as the result of a summer afternoon picnic in the long vacation. He had with him the three children of Dr. Liddell, the pundit mentioned above, the Head of Mr. Dodgson's college, the joint compiler of Liddell and Scott's *Greek Lexicon.* Lewis Carroll has told the story himself.

"I made an expedition up the river," wrote Mr. Dodgson in his diary of July 4, 1862, "to Godstow with the three Liddells; we had tea on the bank there, and did not reach Christ

Church till half-past eight." Later he inserted, "On which occasion I told them the fairy tale of Alice's adventures underground." As a matter of fact, another clerical gentleman, the late Canon Duckworth, says he was also in the boat when Dodgson told the story as they rowed. He may have been. If so, Lewis Carroll forgot he was there. He disappeared like the Cheshire Cat.

So with that we begin to read, or rather we won't begin at the very beginning of the story, for it starts with what is really child stuff—Alice falling down rabbit holes, and biting off bits of mushrooms to get first tall and then small and so on. This hits children hard but not us. . . . Then all of a sudden the story breaks through into such a queer enchanted world of disunited scenery, queer people—and off we go. Let us jump at once into the very best of it—the Mad Hatter's Tea-Party . . .

There was a table set out under a tree in front of the house, and the March Hare and the Hatter were having tea at it: a Dormouse was sitting between them, fast asleep, and the other two were using it as a cushion, resting their elbows on it, and talking over its head. "Very uncomfortable for the Dormouse," thought Alice; "only, as it's asleep, I suppose it doesn't mind."

The table was a large one, but the three were all crowded together at one corner of it: "No room! No room!" they cried out when they saw Alice coming. "There's *plenty* of room!" said Alice indignantly, and she sat down in a large arm-chair at one end of the table.

"Have some wine," the March Hare said in an encouraging tone.

Alice looked all round the table, but there was nothing on it but tea. "I don't see any wine," she remarked.

"There isn't any," said the March Hare.

"Then it wasn't very civil of you to offer it," said Alice angrily.

"It wasn't very civil of you to sit down without being invited," said the March Hare.

"I didn't know it was *your* table," said Alice; "it's laid for a great many more than three."

"Your hair wants cutting," said the Hatter. He had been looking at Alice for some time with great curiosity, and this was his first speech.

"You should learn not to make personal remarks," Alice said with some severity; "it's very rude."

The Hatter opened his eyes very wide on hearing this; but all he *said* was, "Why is a raven like a writing-desk?"

"Come, we shall have some fun now!" thought Alice. "I'm glad they've begun asking riddles—I believe I can guess that," she added aloud.

"Do you mean that you think you can find out the answer to it?" said the March Hare.

"Exactly so," said Alice.

"Then you should say what you mean," the March Hare went on.

"I do," Alice hastily replied; "at least—at least I mean what I say—that's the same thing, you know."

"Not the same thing a bit!" said the Hatter. "Why, you might just as well say that 'I see what I eat' is the same thing as 'I eat what I see'!"

"You might just as well say," added the March Hare, "that 'I like what I get' is the same thing as 'I get what I like'!"

"You might just as well say," added the Dormouse, who seemed to be talking in his sleep, "that 'I breathe when I sleep' is the same thing as 'I sleep when I breathe'!"

"It *is* the same thing with you," said the Hatter, and here the conversation dropped, and the party sat silent for a minute, while Alice thought over all she could remember about ravens and writing-desks, which wasn't much.

The Hatter was the first to break the silence. "What day of the month is it?" he said, turning to Alice; he had taken his watch out of his pocket, and was looking at it uneasily, shaking it every now and then, and holding it to his ear.

Alice considered a little, and then said, "The fourth."

"Two days wrong!" sighed the Hatter. "I told you butter wouldn't suit the works!" he added, looking angrily at the March Hare.

"It was the *best* butter," the March Hare meekly replied.

"Yes, but some crumbs must have got in as well," the Hatter

grumbled: "you shouldn't have put it in with the bread-knife."

The March Hare took the watch and looked at it gloomily: then he dipped it into his cup of tea, and looked at it again: but he could think of nothing better to say than his first remark, "It was the *best* butter, you know."

Now just stop there a moment at that remark, "It was the best butter." That kind of thing—you can't call it exactly a joke, or a quip, or a play upon words, but just a hopelessly inconsequential remark, funny because it sounds as if it ought to mean something and yet it doesn't—that kind of thing occurs and recurs all through the *Wonderland* books, along with the downright puns and plays on words. But these are not the essence of the thing at all. Lewis Carroll would never have got far with that stuff alone. Oddly enough, these are the things that get quoted, but not really for their own sake but for the remembrance of the characters who say them.

But the point is, who are these queer people anyway?— the March Hare and the Mad Hatter and the Dormouse. We don't exactly know. Neither did Lewis Carroll. Sir John Tenniel, the artist, caught from the Hatter the idea of something half-horrible, abnormal, the repulsiveness of blank imbecility. When *Alice in Wonderland* was put on the stage in London, Sydney Harcourt played this kind of Hatter. Lewis Carroll went to see the play and said, "To see him enact the Hatter was a weird and uncanny thing, as though some grotesque monster, seen last night in a dream, should walk into the room in broad daylight and quietly say, 'Good morning.' I need not try to describe what I meant the Hatter to be, since, so far as I can now remember, it was exactly what Mr. Harcourt has made him."

But the Hatter, we must remember, moves in the charm of afternoon sunlight dancing through the leaves on a tea table.

But one can see how these strange characters, splinters of distorted light, hold and fascinate us. They are so exactly like —like what? We don't know.

Alice had been looking over his shoulder with some curiosity. "What a funny watch!" she remarked. "It tells the day of the month, and doesn't tell what o'clock it is!"

"Why should it?" muttered the Hatter. "Does *your* watch tell you what year it is?"

"Of course not," Alice replied very readily: "but that's because it stays the same year for such a long time together."

"Which is just the case with *mine*," said the Hatter.

Alice felt dreadfully puzzled. The Hatter's remark seemed to her to have no sort of meaning in it, and yet it was certainly English. "I don't quite understand you," she said, as politely as she could.

"The Dormouse is asleep again," said the Hatter, and he poured a little hot tea on to its nose.

The Dormouse shook its head impatiently, and said, without opening its eyes, "Of course, of course; just what I was going to remark myself."

"Have you guessed the riddle yet?" the Hatter said, turning to Alice again.

"No, I give it up," Alice replied: "what's the answer?"

"I haven't the slightest idea," said the Hatter.

"Nor I," said the March Hare.

Alice sighed wearily. "I think you might do something better with the time," she said, "than wasting it in asking riddles that have no answers."

"If you knew Time as well as I do," said the Hatter, "you wouldn't talk about wasting *it*. It's *him*."

"I don't know what you mean," said Alice.

"Of course you don't!" the Hatter said, tossing his head contemptuously. "I dare say you never even spoke to Time!"

"Perhaps not," Alice cautiously replied: "but I know I have to beat time when I learn music."

"Ah! that accounts for it," said the Hatter. "He won't stand beating. Now, if you only kept on good terms with him, he'd do almost anything you liked with the clock. For instance, suppose it were nine o'clock in the morning, just time to begin lessons: you'd only have to whisper a hint to Time, and round goes the clock in a twinkling! Half-past one, time for dinner!"

("I only wish it was," the March Hare said to itself in a whisper.)

"That would be grand, certainly," said Alice thoughtfully: "but then—I shouldn't be hungry for it, you know."

"Not at first, perhaps," said the Hatter: "but you could keep it to half-past one as long as you liked."

"Is that the way *you* manage?" Alice asked.

The Hatter shook his head mournfully. "Not I!" he replied. "We quarrelled last March—just before *he* went mad, you know—" (pointing with his teaspoon at the March Hare) "it was at the great concert given by the Queen of Hearts, and I had to sing

'Twinkle, twinkle, little bat!
How I wonder what you're at!'

"You know the song, perhaps?"

"I've heard something like it," said Alice.

"It goes on, you know," the Hatter continued, "in this way:—

'Up above the world you fly,
Like a teatray in the sky.
Twinkle, twinkle—' "

Here the Dormouse shook itself, and began singing in its sleep *"Twinkle, twinkle, twinkle, twinkle—"* and went on so long that they had to pinch it to make it stop.

"Well, I'd hardly finished the first verse," said the Hatter, "when the Queen (jumped up and) bawled out, "He's murdering the time! Off with his head!' "

"How dreadfully savage!" exclaimed Alice.

"And ever since that," the Hatter went on in a mournful tone, "he won't do a thing I ask! It's always six o'clock now."

A bright idea came into Alice's head. "Is that the reason so many tea-things are put out here?" she asked.

"Yes, that's it," said the Hatter with a sigh: "it's always tea-time, and we've no time to wash the things between whiles."

"Then you keep moving round, I suppose?" said Alice.

"Exactly so," said the Hatter: "as the things get used up."

"But what happens when you come to the beginning again?"

Alice ventured to ask.

"Suppose we change the subject," the March Hare interrupted, yawning. "I'm getting tired of this. I vote the young lady tells us a story."

"I'm afraid I don't know one," said Alice, rather alarmed at the proposal.

"Then the Dormouse shall!" they both cried. "Wake up, Dormouse!" And they pinched it on both sides at once.

The Dormouse slowly opened his eyes. "I wasn't asleep," he said in a hoarse, feeble voice: "I heard every word you fellows were saying."

"Tell us a story!" said the March Hare.

"Yes, please do!" pleaded Alice.

"And be quick about it," added the Hatter, "or you'll be asleep again before it's done."

"Once upon a time there were three little sisters," the Dormouse began in a great hurry; "and their names were Elsie, Lacie, and Tillie; and they lived at the bottom of a well—"

"What did they live on?" said Alice, who always took a great interest in questions of eating and drinking.

"They lived on treacle," said the Dormouse, after thinking a minute or two.

"They couldn't have done that, you know," Alice gently remarked: "they'd have been ill."

"So they were," said the Dormouse: "*very* ill."

Alice tried a little to fancy to herself what such an extraordinary way of living would be like, but it puzzled her too much, so she went on: "But why did they live at the bottom of a well?"

"Take some more tea," the March Hare said to Alice, very earnestly.

"I've had nothing yet," Alice replied in an offended tone, "so I can't take more."

"You mean you can't take *less*," said the Hatter: "it's very easy to take *more* than nothing."

"Nobody asked *your* opinion," said Alice.

"Who's making personal remarks now?" the Hatter asked triumphantly.

Alice did not quite know what to say to this: so she helped herself to some tea and bread-and-butter, and then turned to the

Dormouse, and repeated her question. "Why did they live at the bottom of a well?"

The Dormouse again took a minute or two to think about it, and then said, "It was a treacle-well."

"There's no such thing!" Alice was beginning very angrily, but the Hatter and the March Hare went "Sh! sh!" and the Dormouse sulkily remarked, "If you can't be civil, you'd better finish the story for yourself."

"No, please go on!" Alice said very humbly: "I won't interrupt you again. I dare say there may be *one*."

"One, indeed!" said the Dormouse indignantly. However, he consented to go on. "And so these three little sisters—they were learning to draw, you know—"

What did they draw?" said Alice, quite forgetting her promise.

"Treacle," said the Dormouse, without considering at all this time.

"I want a clean cup," interrupted the Hatter "let's all move one place on."

He moved on as he spoke, and the Dormouse followed him: the March Hare moved into the Dormouse's place, and Alice rather unwillingly took the place of the March Hare. The Hatter was the only one who got any advantage from the change: and Alice was a good deal worse off than before, as the March Hare had just upset the milk-jug into his plate.

Alice did not wish to offend the Dormouse again, so she began very cautiously: "But I don't understand. Where did they draw the treacle from?"

"You can draw water out of a water-well," said the Hatter; "so I should think you could draw treacle out of a treacle-well—eh, stupid?"

"But they were *in* the well," Alice said to the Dormouse, not choosing to notice this last remark.

"Of course they were," said the Dormouse,—"well in."

This answer so confused poor Alice, that she let the Dormouse go on for some time without interrupting it.

"They were learning to draw," the Dormouse went on, yawning and rubbing its eyes, for it was getting very sleepy; "and they drew all manner of things—everything that begins with an M—"

"Why with an M?" said Alice.

"Why not?" said the March Hare.

Alice was silent.

The Dormouse had closed its eyes by this time, and was going off into a doze; but, on being pinched by the Hatter, it woke up again with a little shriek, and went on: "—that begins with an M, such as mousetraps, and the moon, and memory, and muchness—you know you say things are 'much of a muchness'—did you ever see such a thing as a drawing of a muchness?"

"Really, now you ask me," said Alice, very much confused, "I don't think—"

"Then you shouldn't talk," said the Hatter.

This piece of rudeness was more than Alice could bear: she got up in great disgust, and walked off; the Dormouse fell asleep instantly, and neither of the others took the least notice of her going, though she looked back once or twice, half hoping that they would call after her: the last time she saw them, they were trying to put the Dormouse into the teapot.

So Alice "wonders on" and all of a sudden here are two more of these queer characters appearing in the strange, inconsequential scene that shifts from minute to minute. Here are Tweedledum and Tweedledee.

They were standing under a tree, each with an arm round the other's neck, and Alice knew which was which in a moment, because one of them had "DUM" embroidered on his collar, and the other "DEE." "I suppose they've each got "TWEEDLE" round at the back of the collar," she said to herself.

They stood so still that she quite forgot they were alive, and she was just looking round to see if the word "TWEEDLE" was written at the back of each collar, when she was startled by a voice coming from the one marked "DUM."

"If you think we're wax-works," he said, "you ought to pay, you know. Wax-works weren't made to be looked at for nothing. Nohow!"

"Contrariwise," added the one marked "DEE," "if you think we're alive, you ought to speak."

"I'm sure I'm very sorry," was all Alice could say; for the words of the old song kept ringing through her head like the ticking of a clock, and she could hardly help saying them out aloud:

> "Tweedledum and Tweedledee
> Agreed to have a battle;
> For Tweedledum said Tweedledee
> Had spoiled his nice new rattle.

> "Just then flew down a monstrous crow,
> As black as a tar-barrel;
> Which frightened both the heroes so,
> They quite forgot their quarrel."

"I know what you're thinking about," said Tweedledum: "but it isn't so, nohow."

"Contrariwise," continued Tweedledee, "if it was so, it might be; and if it were so, it would be: but as it isn't, it ain't. That's logic."

We realize at once the fascination of Tweedledum and Tweedledee, so alike and yet different. They stand for the "two-ness" of things, all that results from things being two and two, either two and two in contrast, or two and two in agreement. Nothing is complete without the something that goes with it. Tweedledum implies tweedledee. There is a metaphysical theory for this, something about thesis and antithesis, but call it Tweedledum and Tweedledee and it's easier.

There is more to it than this. Tweedledum and tweedledee represent academic reasoning, college argument. "If it were so, it would be; but as it isn't, it ain't." . . . Any third year class in logic will feel something stir in them at that. This aspect of academic reasoning reappears as soon as Tweedledee, at his brother's request (notice how they work together), recites for Alice the most famous of all the Lewis Carroll poems (except perhaps the *Jabberwocky*), *The Walrus and the Carpenter*. These interpolated poems were in accord with the fashion of the day and don't, of necessity, follow the character of the reciter. But in this case they do. We must not quote the whole poem here, but observe:

"The Walrus and the Carpenter
Were walking close at hand;
They wept like anything to see
Such quantities of sand:
'If this were only cleared away,'
They said, 'it *would* be grand!

" 'If seven maids with seven mops
Swept it for half a year;
Do you suppose,' the Walrus said,
'That they could get it clear?'
'I doubt it,' said the Carpenter,
And shed a bitter tear."

We note here the queer half-suggestion of statistics and mathematics; the exact calculation of the seven maids with seven mops working for six months, followed by the feeble mathematical conclusion, "I doubt it." There is, of course, no room for doubt in mathematics; either they do it or they don't. But this queer, sudden collapse of what sounded like severe reasoning, sounds terribly like something—is it parliamentary finance? or what?

The collegiate note is struck even more strongly a little lower down. Anybody who has ever looked over the thing called the agenda of a scientific society, meaning the mixture of things they propose to talk about, will recognize at once the type.

" 'The time has come,' the Walrus said,
'To talk of many things:
Of shoes—and ships—and sealing-wax—
Of cabbages—and kings—
And why the sea is boiling hot—
And whether pigs have wings.' "

The concluding verses, however, break away from mathematics and rest on problems of what seem to be mutual service and social help—but end (again just like something or other) in the death of the oysters.

" 'It was so kind of you to come!
    And you are very nice!'
The Carpenter said nothing but
    'Cut us another slice:
I wish you were not quite so deaf—
    I've had to ask you twice!'

" 'It seems a shame,' the Walrus said,
    'To play them such a trick,
After we've brought them out so far,
    And made them trot so quick!'
The Carpenter said nothing but
    'The butter's spread too thick!'

" 'I weep for you,' the Walrus said:
    'I deeply sympathize.'
With sobs and tears he sorted out
    Those of the largest size,
Holding his pocket-handkerchief
    Before his streaming eyes.

" 'O Oysters,' said the Carpenter,
    'You've had a pleasant run!
Shall we be trotting home again?'
    But answer came there none—
And this was scarcely odd, because
    They'd eaten every one."

On the conclusion of the recitation, Tweedledum and Tweedledee apply college reasoning to the Carpenter and the Walrus—what is called in philosophy the problem of conduct.

"I like the Walrus best," said Alice: "because you see he was a *little* sorry for the poor oysters."

"He ate more than the Carpenter, though," said Tweedledee. "You see, he held his handkerchief in front, so that the Carpenter couldn't count how many he took: contrariwise."

"That was mean!" Alice said indignantly. "Then I like the Carpenter best—if he didn't eat so many as the Walrus."

"But he ate as many as he could get," said Tweedledum.

The characters come drifting past—the White Queen who turns into a Sheep, Humpty Dumpty who lives in a tangle of Arithmetic, Kings, Lions and Unicorns, and then round the corner we go, right into the Middle Ages with the Red Knight and the White Knight. After their terrific duel, the Red Knight gallops off and Alice is left alone with the White Knight. One can picture him! His queer accoutrement of tin pans and "inventions" hung all around him; his gentle, simple face; his easy acceptance of failure; his refusal to complain; his willingness, if need be, to talk upside-down . . . Cervantes in his *Don Quixote* painted a picture of departing chivalry, laughing it off the stage of history, as it were, only to find it come back again at his call. Mark Twain transported his Connecticut Yankee to King Arthur's Court, to show what invention could do for mediaeval stagnation. But Lewis Carroll in *Alice in Wonderland*, even before the *Yankee* was written, had joined him with Don Quixote into the beautiful character of the White Knight, the character of "God's Fool" that appears and reappears in the world's literature. We may read him straight ahead for he interprets himself as he goes.

"It was a glorious victory, wasn't it?" said the White Knight, as he came up panting.

"I don't know," Alice said doubtfully. "I don't want to be anybody's prisoner. I want to be a Queen."

"So you will, when you've crossed the next brook," said the White Knight. "I'll see you safe to the end of the wood—and then I must go back, you know. That's the end of my move."

"Thank you very much," said Alice. "May I help you off with your helmet?" It was evidently more than he could manage by himself; however, she managed to shake him out of it at last.

"Now one can breathe more easily," said the Knight, putting back his shaggy hair with both hands, and turning his gentle face and large mild eyes to Alice. She thought she had never seen such a strange-looking soldier in all her life.

He was dressed in tin armour, which seemed to fit him very

badly, and he had a queer little deal box fastened across his shoulders upside-down, and with the lid hanging open. Alice looked at it with great curiosity.

"I see you're admiring my little box," the Knight said in a friendly tone. "It's my own invention—to keep clothes and sandwiches in. You see, I carry it upside-down, so that the rain can't get in."

"But the things can get *out*," Alice gently remarked. "Do you know the lid's open?"

"I didn't know it," the Knight said, a shade of vexation passing over his face. "Then all the things must have fallen out! And the box is no use without them." He unfastened it as he spoke, and was just going to throw it into the bushes, when a sudden thought seemed to strike him, and he hung it carefully on a tree. "Can you guess why I did that?" he said to Alice.

Alice shook her head.

"In hopes some bees may make a nest in it—then I should get the honey."

"But you've got a bee-hive—or something like one—fastened to the saddle," said Alice.

"Yes, it's a very good bee-hive," the Knight said in a discontented tone, "one of the best kind. But not a single bee has come near it yet. And the other thing is a mouse-trap. I suppose the mice keep the bees out—or the bees keep the mice out, I don't know which."

"I was wondering what the mouse-trap was for," said Alice. "It isn't very likely there would be any mice on the horse's back."

"Not very likely, perhaps," said the Knight; "but if they *do* come, I don't choose to have them running all about."

"You see," he went on after a pause, "it's as well to be provided for *everything*. That's the reason the horse has anklets round his feet."

"But what are they for?" Alice asked in a tone of great curiosity.

"To guard against the bites of sharks," the Knight replied. "It's an invention of my own. And now help me on. I'll go with you to the end of the wood. What's that dish for?"

"It's meant for plum-cake," said Alice.

"We'd better take it with us," the Knight said. "It'll come in handy if we find any plum-cake. Help me to get it into this bag."

This took a long time to manage, though Alice held the bag open very carefully, because the Knight was so *very* awkward in putting in the dish: the first two or three times that he tried he fell in himself instead. "It's rather a tight fit, you see," he said, as they got it in at last; "there are so many candlesticks in the bag." And he hung it to the saddle, which was already loaded with bunches of carrots, and fire-irons, and many other things.

"I hope you've got your hair well fastened on?" he continued, as they set off.

"Only in the usual way," Alice said, smiling.

"That's hardly enough," he said anxiously. "You see, the wind is so *very* strong here. It's as strong as soup."

"Have you invented a plan for keeping one's hair from being blown off?" Alice inquired.

"Not yet," said the Knight. "But I've got a plan for keeping it from *falling* off."

"I should like to hear it very much."

"First you take an upright stick," said the Knight. "Then you make your hair creep up it, like a fruit-tree. Now the reason hair falls off is because it hangs *down*—things never fall *upwards*, you know. It's my own invention. You may try it if you like."

It didn't sound a comfortable plan, Alice thought, and for a few minutes she walked on in silence, puzzling over the idea, and every now and then stopping to help the poor Knight, who certainly was *not* a good rider.

Whenever the horse stopped (which it did very often), he fell off in front; and whenever it went on again (which it generally did rather suddenly), he fell off behind. Otherwise he kept on pretty well, except that he had a habit of now and then falling off sideways; and as he generally did this on the side on which Alice was walking, she soon found that it was the best plan not to walk *quite* close to the horse.

"I'm afraid you've not had much practice in riding," she ventured to say, as she was helping him up from his fifth tumble.

The Knight looked very much surprised, and a little offended at the remark. "What makes you say that?" he asked, as he scrambled back into the saddle, keeping hold of Alice's hair with one hand, to save himself from falling over on the other side.

"Because people don't fall off quite so often, when they've had much practice."

"I've had plenty of practice," the Knight said very gravely; "plenty of practice!"

Alice could think of nothing better to say than "Indeed?" but she said it as heartily as she could. They went on a little way in silence after this, the Knight with his eyes shut, muttering to himself, and Alice watched anxiously for the next tumble.

"The great art of riding," the Knight suddenly began in a loud voice, waving his right arm as he spoke, "is to keep—" Here the sentence ended as suddenly as it had begun, as the Knight fell heavily on the top of his head exactly in the path where Alice was walking. She was quite frightened this time, and said in an anxious tone, as she picked him up, "I hope no bones are broken?"

"None to speak of," the Knight said, as if he didn't mind breaking two or three of them. "The great art of riding, as I was saying, is—to keep your balance. Like this, you know—"

He let go the bridle, and stretched out both his arms to show Alice what he meant, and this time he fell flat on his back, right under the horse's feet.

"Plenty of practice!" he went on repeating, all the time that Alice was getting him on his feet again. "Plenty of practice!"

"It's too ridiculous!" cried Alice, getting quite out of patience. "You ought to have a wooden horse on wheels, that you ought!"

"Does that kind go smoothly?" the Knight asked in a tone of great interest, clasping his arms round the horse's neck as he spoke, just in time to save himself from tumbling off again.

"Much more smoothly than a live horse," Alice said, with a little scream of laughter, in spite of all she could do to prevent it.

"I'll get one," the Knight said thoughtfully to himself. "One or two—several."

There was a short silence after this; then the Knight went on again. "I'm a great hand at inventing things. Now, I daresay you noticed, the last time you picked me up, that I was looking thoughtful?"

"You *were* a little grave," said Alice.

"Well, just then I was inventing a new way of getting over a gate—would you like to hear it?"

"Very much indeed," Alice said politely.

"I'll tell you how I came to think of it," said the Knight. "You see, I said to myself, 'The only difficulty is with the feet; the *head* is high enough already.' Now, first I put my head on the top of the gate—then the head's high enough—then I stand on my head—then the feet are high enough, you see—then I'm over, you see."

"Yes, I suppose you'd be over when that was done," Alice said thoughtfully; "but don't you think it would be rather hard?"

"I haven't tried it yet," the Knight said gravely: "so I can't tell for certain—but I'm afraid it *would* be a little hard."

He looked so vexed at the idea that Alice changed the subject hastily. "What a curious helmet you've got!" she said cheerfully. "Is that your invention too?"

The Knight looked down proudly at his helmet, which hung from the saddle. "Yes," he said, "but I've invented a better one than that—like a sugar-loaf. When I used to wear it, if I fell off the horse, it always touched the ground directly. So I had a *very* little way to fall, you see. But there *was* the danger of falling *into* it, to be sure. That happened to me once—and the worst of it was, before I could get out again, the other White Knight came and put it on. He thought it was his own helmet."

The Knight looked so solemn about it that Alice did not dare to laugh. "I'm afraid you must have hurt him," she said in a trembling voice, "being on the top of his head."

"I had to kick him, of course," the Knight said, very seriously. "And then he took the helmet off again—but it took hours and hours to get me out. I was as fast as—as lightning, you know."

"But that's a different kind of fastness," Alice objected.

The Knight shook his head. "It was all kinds of fastness with me, I can assure you!" he said. He raised his hands in some excitement as he said this, and instantly rolled out of the saddle, and fell headlong into a deep ditch.

Alice ran to the side of the ditch to look for him. She was rather startled by the fall, as for some time he had kept on very well, and she was afraid that he really *was* hurt this time. However, though she could see nothing but the soles of his feet, she was much relieved to hear that he was talking on in his usual tone. "All kinds of fastness," he repeated; "but it was careless of him to put another man's helmet on—with the man in it, too."

"How *can* you go on talking so quietly, head downwards?" Alice asked, as she dragged him out by the feet, and laid him in a heap on the bank.

The Knight looked surprised at the question. "What does it matter where my body happens to be?" he said. "My mind goes on working all the same. In fact, the more head downwards I am, the more I keep inventing new things."

"Now the cleverest thing that I ever did," he went on after a pause, "was inventing a new pudding during the meat-course."

"In time to have it cooked for the next course?" said Alice. "Well, that *was* quick work, certainly."

"Well, not the *next* course," the Knight said in a slow thoughtful tone; "no, certainly not the next *course.*"

"Then it would have to be the next day. I suppose you wouldn't have two pudding-courses in one dinner?"

"Well, not the *next* day," the Knight repeated as before: "not the next *day*. In fact," he went on, holding his head down, and his voice getting lower and lower, "I don't believe that pudding ever *was* cooked! In fact, I don't believe that pudding ever *will* be cooked! And yet it was a very clever pudding to invent."

"What did you mean it to be made of?" Alice asked, hoping to cheer him up, for he seemed quite low-spirited about it.

"It began with blotting-paper," the Knight answered with a groan.

"That wouldn't be very nice, I'm afraid—"

"Not very nice *alone*," he interrupted, quite eagerly; "but you've no idea what a difference it makes, mixing it with other things—such as gunpowder and sealing-wax. And here I must leave you."

Alice in Wonderland, as we have seen, came together by a sort of mystical gathering of bits and scraps, of ideas that came of themselves. As a result, by a sort of mathematical paradox, the whole turned out to be greater than its parts. Lewis Carroll himself, somewhat perplexed at this, wrote, "Words mean more than we mean to express when we use them; so a whole book ought to mean a great deal more than the writer means," nor was he trying to be funny when he said it. The proof of this is found in the fact that when he tried to repeat the process deliberately he failed utterly. The result of this attempt was embodied in the unhappy trash called *Sylvie and Bruno*, published in 1889. It met a hollow and false acclaim and rapidly subsided into oblivion. The book has long since been forgiven and forgotten. Here again are little children in a garden, one of them a boy—or meant to be. Lewis Carroll was not strong on boys. Indeed, his admiring biographer, Mr. Stuart Collingwood of Christ Church, calmly tells us that "he professed an aversion to boy nature, almost amounting to terror." So little Bruno may have been born wrong by reason of Lewis Carroll's fright. The book *Sylvie and Bruno* is meant to be another *Wonderland*, with the same queer shifting scenes and odd characters. But it doesn't work. This time Lewis Carroll had gone at it deliberately. For years, we are told, he jotted down little actual scraps of child conversation. This was especially for Bruno who is at the baby stage and says "OO" for *you*. . . . "Does oo always confuses two animals together?" asks Bruno. "Oo never believes me," he complains. Another time he says, "I never talks to nobody when he isn't here. Oo should always wait till he comes before oo talks to him." Pretty cute, eh? Don't oo think so? In fact, about as tiresome as are all the quoted sayings of little children—except one's own. Indeed, one would feel inclined to hand Bruno over to the Duchess and let him turn into a pig.

Ever so many people have tried to imitate Lewis Carroll and failed. But the first one who tried and failed was Lewis Carroll himself.

Gilbert's "Bab" Ballads

It is a great change from the secluded woodland of *Wonderland* to the open scenes, the noise and the combat of the *"Bab" Ballads*. Here are the breezes of the sea, the thunder of guns, the clash of swords and the thud of the executioner's axe. In Alice's *Wonderland*, the characters just fade away and disappear. In the *"Bab" Ballads*, they are thrown into the sea, knocked on the head, or cut clean in two with scimitars of exquisite sharpness and their remains fed to sharks or boiled up by enthusiastic cannibals. In the most "popular" of the ballads, meaning the one that the plain people have liked best, *The Yarn of the "Nancy Bell,"* one character eats all the others, one by one. "Mr. Gilbert," says a penetrating critic of today, "shows a sort of cruelty. . . . In fact, he cared little about the feelings of others." Very little, one would think, if he boiled them alive and chopped them up, as one famous ballad puts it, "particularly small." The same critic, however, adds that Gilbert was a "full-blooded, impatient Englishman," which explains the whole thing.

But there are other differences between *Wonderland* and the *Balladland*: the people in *Wonderland* have no names. They are all generalizations—the Mad Hatter, the Red Queen, or fictions like Humpty Dumpty and Tweedledee. But in the *Ballads* they are all real people, with names and rank. Here are Captain Reece, R.N., and Captain Parklebury Todd; here is the Reverend Simon Magus—people you might meet in London any day. The scholarly world is represented by Gregory Parable, LL.D., and here is little Annie Profterie who kept a small post office in the neighbourhood of Bow—just what she would naturally do. Any one guesses at once, as Gilbert admitted in advance, that Macphairson Clonglocketty Angus McClan was a Scotchman. The whole setting is intended to show that we are dealing with real life, simply presented. Even the outsiders, not English, are equally convincing. Alum Bey is a proper Turk. The name of King Borria Bungalee Boo certainly indicates him as a "man-eating African swell." Yet in spite of all these features of normality, these home touches, so to speak, the world of Gilbert's *"Bab" Ballads* is just as topsy-turvy as the world of Alice's *Wonderland*.

Let us see how it originated.

The name of W. S. Gilbert is known to most people today only as the larger half of Gilbert and Sullivan, a combination now as familiar as Damon and Pythias or Lea and Perrins. But, in reality, Gilbert had already achieved quite a celebrity in London before the resounding and prolonged triumph of the Savoy Operas.

W. S. Gilbert (1836-1911) was born a gentleman—a matter that must have been a permanent satisfaction to him. His father was a surgeon in the Royal Navy and later a novelist, a fiery, peppery old gentleman who went around trying to give editors a thrashing and offering to throw people out of the window—in short, right out of the *"Bab" Ballads* alongside of Captain Parklebury Todd who "couldn't walk into a room without ejaculating, 'Boom!'" Gilbert went to the kind of private school called, in England, a public school, and was to have been sent up, or down, whichever it is, to Oxford. But the outbreak of the Crimean War led him to take a quicker training at King's College, London, in order to get a commission in the army. Just as he finished it, the war ended. So Gilbert got neither Oxford nor war and turned off sideways to the bar. At the bar he acquired that wealth of legal phrases which adorned all his works and broke into song again and again in the operas—"When I went to the bar-as-a-very-young-man, said I to myself, said I."

Gilbert had, in all, twenty clients in five years. One, a

Frenchman, acquitted, threw his arms around Gilbert's neck in court and kissed him. Another, a woman pickpocket, convicted, threw her book at him in disgust. Another, an Irishman, prosecuted by him, kept shouting, "Sit down, ye devil, sit down!"

So Gilbert gave up the law and turned to art and humour and was an immediate success. His mock-heroic ballads and the drawings he made for them became the leading feature of *Fun*, the new comic journal that was running *Punch* hard in the Sixties. They were signed *Bab*, which had been a childish nickname for Gilbert himself, and so when published as a book, they appeared as the *"Bab" Ballads*—first in 1869, and then enlarged, and reprinted, and recollected and so around the world.

Hence W. S. Gilbert was already quite a celebrity in London long before the Gilbert and Sullivan operas turned celebrity to glory. But in a way it was not altogether an enviable celebrity. Gilbert from all accounts was a singularly disagreeable man, self-important and domineering, rating everybody else as poor trash. By good rights, great humourists ought to be gentle, agreeable people to meet, with a breadth of view and a kindly tolerance of trifles—such as they show in print. Mostly they are not. Charles Dickens, in spite of a boundless energy and exuberance of fun, was an intolerable egotist who had to be "it" all the time, who supplied sob-words and slow music for the fathers of broken homes and smashed his own with an axe. Mark Twain, though good, easy company when young, became, so some people tell us, intolerably boring in old age. Lewis Carroll was a sissy, and Gilbert was a bully, over-conscious of his own talent.

Thus Gilbert used his, this singular talent, to point the barbs of his retorts and jokes. Very funny to read, they are, these retorts and repartee. But some of them must have cut people to the heart.

"What did you think of my Hamlet?" asked an actor friend in the first flush of his pride in his new part. . . . "Excellent," said Gilbert, "funny all through, but never vulgar."

A barber cutting Gilbert's hair once bent over his ear to murmur, "When are we to expect anything further, Mr. Gilbert, from your fluent pen?"

"What do you mean, sir, by fluent pen?" snapped Gilbert. "There is no such thing as a fluent pen. A pen is an insensible object. And, at any rate, I don't presume to enquire into your private affairs; you will please observe the same reticence in regard to mine."

Any one who could thus snub a barber out of his one privilege, would strike a child . . . though, as a matter of fact, Gilbert wouldn't. He was friendly and companionable with children, just as he was an excellent host and a generous supporter of charitable things. He kept his quarrels for his own world, and for the law courts, where he lived in litigation. . . . "The judge," he said, in writing of one of his lost actions, "summed up like a drunken monkey. He's in the last stage of senile decay." After Sir Edward Carson won a case against him, Gilbert made a point of cutting him dead.

As a result, Gilbert's life was filled with bitter quarrels. There were some people he wouldn't speak to for ten years; others were on the twenty-year list. As his old age drew on, a strange repentance seized him, especially as the former friends, put on the silent list, began to pass into a silence longer still. As each died, Gilbert was all contrition, with flowers sent to hospitals, looking for old ties to rebind, the egotism all paled out of him. He could have made a wonderful *Ballad* out of it—*The Contrite Playwright*.

But all that was far away at the time of which we speak.

But to understand the *"Bab" Ballads* we need not only to understand Gilbert himself but to see in its proper perspective the period in which he wrote.

This was the period of the Great Peace, after 1815, that was going to last forever; everybody knew it, and the Crystal Palace proved it. There might be wars as a matter of distant adventure, like the Crimean War; or wars in suitable out-of-the-way places like Ashantee; and among crazy European revolutionists. But, for England, war had been removed forever by Trafalgar and Waterloo. There sat the right little tight little island, snug behind the waves, and you couldn't get at it. "The English," wrote a very witty person of the time in referring to the new misty German philosophy, "are supreme on the sea, the French on the land, and the Germans hold the supremacy of the air." How strange it sounds now.

In this safeness and snugness, with outside protection and internal order and personal liberty guaranteed, all values shifted. The things that seemed so vital before—religion that people burned for, liberty that people hanged for, defence that people died for—began to be taken for granted. They were all embodied in the policeman, the magistrate, the M.P. and the justices of the peace. With the sole proviso of keeping the poor in the proper place, if need be by shooting them, the government had nothing to do. Hence the whole apparatus of government, British constitution and all, began to seem amazingly funny, especially because of all its forms and its feathers and its fuss, its Beef-eaters and Yeomen of the Guard.

In fact, to clever men like young Dickens and young Gilbert, it was really a huge joke, just a scream. Take the Royal Family, with its multiplying household and its German regularity and parsimony.

The Queen she kept high festival in Windsor's lofty hall,
And round her sat her gartered knights and ermined nobles all,
There drank the valiant Wellington, there fed the Wary Peel,
While at the bottom of the board Prince Albert carved the veal.

Carved the veal! Pretty funny, eh? And, of course, the statesmen and the cabinet, chasing one another in and out of office, were just as funny—what was it Dickens called them? Coodle, and Doodle and Foodle! . . . and the Members of Parliament always making speeches and laying their hands on their heart! . . . and the army, now there *is* something to laugh at! all drooping plumes and dangling swords! What did they think they were out to kill anyway? And the House of Lords, all in robes doing nothing, and the clergy all in gaiters doing less. Let's have a song about the House of Lords which, throughout the War, did nothing in particular and did it rather well! And let's make up comic verses about the Bishop of Rum-ti-Foo.

All these things seemed out of date! We can see it all better now. A generation that has seen the world swept back into barbarism by two world wars can see reality again. Why, these mean the things—this funny Parliament, this comic magistrate, even Coodle and Doodle—the things that people die for.

But not being able to see it, the world seemed all topsy-turvy.

We left out the navy above. Was it comic or real? They weren't quite sure. The sea lies close to the British heart. Even Gilbert was an amateur Yo-ho yachtsman of the coast. Hence the England of this epoch never knew whether to admire the navy, or to laugh at it like the army. And the government never knew whether to improve its lot and feed and warm it decently or whether to "give it every day at least six dozen lashes," as Gilbert gave to Joe Golightly.

So Gilbert took the navy both ways. Here belongs tne famous ballad of *Captain Reece*, Commander of *The Mantelpiece* that turned later on into the opera *Pinafore*. Captain Reece represents that fatal pelting of the seamen under the new philanthropy in which the real old blue-water school saw the approaching downfall of England, the scuttling of the ship.

CAPTAIN REECE

Of all the ships upon the blue,
No ship contained a better crew
Than that of worthy Captain Reece,
Commanding of *The Mantelpiece*.

He was adored by all his men,
For worthy Captain Reece, R.N.,
Did all that lay within him to
Promote the comfort of his crew.

If ever they were dull or sad,
Their captain danced to them like mad,
Or told, to make the time pass by,
Droll legends of his infancy.

A feather bed had every man,
Warm slippers and hot-water can,
Brown windsor from the captain's store,
A valet, too, to every four.

Did they with thirst in summer burn?
Lo, seltzogenes at every turn,
And on all very sultry days
Cream ices handed round on trays.

Kind-hearted Captain Reece, R.N.,
Was quite devoted to his men;
In point of fact, good Captain Reece,
Beatified *The Mantelpiece*.

This idyllic situation culminated in the happy idea of marrying all the crew to Captain Reece's sisters cousins and aunts. Even the captain was not forgotten.

The boatswain of *The Mantelpiece*,
He blushed and spoke to Captain Reece:
"I beg your honour's leave," he said,
"If you would wish to go and wed,

"I have a widowed mother who
Would be the very thing for you—
She long has loved you from afar,
She washes for you, Captain R."

And the curtain falls on a happy and united family crew. Such a picture must have another side. The navy was not all human kindliness and new philanthropy. There was still the same old brutality to denounce where some ferocious martinet got his evil way, flogging his crew into submission. Tennyson denounced this in his own melodramatic way; Gilbert showed how topsy-turvy it was; in fact turned it into fun. Which helped more to abolish it?

Tennyson begins:

> He that only rules by terror
> Doth a grievous wrong,
> Deep as hell I count his error.
> Let him hear my song.

and goes on to tell of a brutal ship's captain whose men took vengeance on him in a naval engagement by curling up and dying on the deck without fighting. It sounds a little bit like the Chinese system of getting even with an enemy by committing suicide on his doorstep.

Now let us see how Gilbert does it. The Admiralty have heard about *The Mantelpiece* and are horrified at Reece's leniency. A new commander, Sir Berkely, a martinet is sent to take over:

> Sir Berkely was a martinet—
> A stern, unyielding soul—
> Who ruled his ship by dint of whip
> And horrible black-hole.
>
> When first Sir Berkely came aboard
> He read a speech to all,
> And told them how he'd made a vow
> To act on duty's call.
>
> Then William Lee, he up and said
> (The Captain's coxswain he):
> "We've heard the speech your honour's made,
> And werry pleased we be.
>
> "We don't pretend, my lad, as how
> We're glad to lose our Reece;

Urbane, polite, he suited quite
  The saucy *Mantelpiece*.

"But if your honour gives your mind
  To study all our ways,
With dance and song we'll jog along
  As in those happy days.

"I like your honour's looks, and feel
  You're worthy of your sword.
Your hand, my lad—I'm doosid glad
  To welcome you aboard!"

Sir Berkely looked amazed, as though
  He didn't understand.
"Don't shake your head," good William said,
  "It is an honest hand.

"It's grasped a better hand than yourn—
  Come, gov'nor, I insist!"
The Captain stared—the coxswain glared—
  The hand became a fist!

"Down, upstart!" said the hardy salt;
  But Berkely dodged his aim,
And made him go in chains below:
  The seamen murmured "Shame!"

A sailor who was overcome
  From having freely dined,
And chanced to reel when at the wheel,
  He instantly confined!

And tars who, when an action raged,
  Appeared alarmed or scared,
And those below who wished to go,
  He very seldom spared.

E'en he who smote his officer
  For punishment was booked,
And mutinies upon the seas
  He rarely overlooked.

> In short, the happy *Mantelpiece*
> Where all had gone so well,
> Beneath that fool Sir Berkely's rule
> Became a floating hell.

This intolerable situation very naturally led the crew to shoot Sir Berkely. The Admiralty on hearing the news of his death realized the wrong that had been done and restored the noble Reece to his command.

But Gilbert's topsy-turvy navy would, of course, not be complete without a picture of the life and sorrows of the common seaman. This is given to us in the pathetic story of Joe Golightly, who had fallen hopelessly in love at a distance, an immeasurable social distance, with the daughter of the First Lord of the Admiralty. Having no other way to voice his love, Joe sang it on board his ship to the mournful thrumming of a guitar:

> *The moon is on the sea,*
> > *Willow!*
> *The wind blows towards the lee,*
> > *Willow!*
> *But though I sigh and sob and cry,*
> *No Lady Jane for me,*
> > *Willow!*
> *She says, " 'Twere folly quite,*
> > *Willow!*
> *For me to wed a wight,*
> > *Willow!*
> *Whose lot is cast before the mast;"*
> *And possibly she's right,*
> > *Willow!*

> His skipper (Captain Joyce)
> > He gave him many a rating,
> And almost lost his voice
> > From thus expostulating:

> "Lay out, you lubber, do!
> > What's come to that young man, Joe?

Belay!—'vast heaving! you!
  Do kindly stop that banjo!

"I wish, I do—oh, Lor'!—
  You'd shipped aboard a trader:
Are you a sailor, or
  A negro serenader?"

But still the stricken cad,
  Aloft or on his pillow,
Howled forth in accents sad
  His aggravating "Willow!"

Stern love of duty had
  Been Joyce's chiefest beauty:
Says he, "I love that lad,
  But duty, damme! duty!

"Twelve years' black-hole, I say,
  Where daylight never flashes;
And always twice a day
  Five hundred thousand lashes!"

But Joseph had a mate,
  A sailor stout and lusty,
A man of low estate,
  But singularly trusty.

Says he, "Cheer hup, young Joe,
  I'll tell you what I'm arter,
To that Fust Lord I'll go
  And ax him for his darter.

"To that Fust Lord I'll go
  And say you love her dearly."
And Joe said (weeping low),
  "I wish you would, sincerely!"

That sailor to that Lord
  Went, soon as he had landed,
And of his own accord
  An interview demanded.

Says he, with seaman's roll,
"My Captain (wot's a Tartar)
Guv Joe twelve years' black-hole,
For lovering your darter.

"He loves Miss Lady Jane
(I own she is his betters),
But if you'll jine them twain,
They'll free him from his fetters.

"And if so be as how
You'll let her come aboard ship,
I'll take her with me now."—
"Get out!" remarked his Lordship.

That honest tar repaired
To Joe, upon the billow,
And told him how he'd fared:
Joe only whispered, "Willow!"

And for that dreadful crime
(Young sailors, learn to shun it)
He's working out his time:
In ten years he'll have done it.

The most celebrated of all the nautical ballads is the one mentioned above, *The Yarn of the "Nancy Bell."* It is a ballad of shipwrecked sailors, as sung by the solitary survivor. They had been driven to cannibalism and had eaten one another, one by one, till only this man is left but he, as he himself says, embodies all the others. The topic is certainly gruesome, yet it was thought roaring fun for half a century. It became a standing literary reproach against Mark Lemon, the editor of *Punch*, that when Gilbert wrote *The Yarn of the "Nancy Bell,"* he wouldn't accept it. The joke was supposed to be that the editor of *Punch*, of all papers, didn't know humour when he saw it. Looking back on it, we don't feel so sure. Gruesome things, if they are to be humorous, must never show actual detail. We remember Lear's comic pictures in which people are cut neatly into halves, but of course with no trace of blood, and no sign of emotion except surprise. We recall out of *Alice in Wonderland* how in the Jabberwocky poem:

> One, two. One, two. And through and through
> The vorpal blade went snicker-snack.
> He left it dead, and with its head
> He went galumphing back.

But Gilbert in the *Nancy Bell* not only puts in details that won't bear actual visualization, but seems, so to speak, to "feature" them; this is especially true of the climax of the poem; only two survivors are left—the cook, naturally kept as long as possible by acclamation, and one seaman. The cook prepares the boiling pot.

> . . . He boils the water, and takes the salt
> And the pepper in portions true
> (Which he never forgot), and some chopped shalot,
> And some sage and parsley too.

That's all right. We can stand for them because it isn't real. It's as harmless as Mark Twain's *Cannibalism in the Cars*. But notice what follows. The surviving sailor steals a march on the cook and tips him into the pot.

> And he stirred it round and round and round,
> And he sniffed at the foaming froth;
> When I ups with his heels, and smothers his squeals
> In the scum of the boiling broth.

> And I ate that cook in a week or less,
> And—as I eating be
> The last of his chops, why, I almost drops,
> For a vessel in sight I see.

The survivor is saved, but at the price of an internal burden that weighs him down forever.

The poem, I say, seemed great fun to a whole generation and more. I remember hearing it read aloud at a country schoolchildren's entertainment in darkest Ontario in 1878. It called forth rounds of laughter. The more they ate one another the better we liked it. Not so now. I think the Great War killed the *Nancy Bell*—the new actuality of the horrors and sufferings of the sea, of the agonies of wounded men thirsting or starving in open boats—no, the topic is off.

Very different is Mark Twain's *Cannibalism in the Cars,* as accomplished by a group of western congressmen, snowed in by a mountain blizzard—but done with the scrupulous regard for legislature procedure that robs it of all offence.

After the navy came the Church. Mr. Gilbert's cruel tendency to make fun of bishops and curates had broken out long before Lewis Carroll complained of the *Pale Young Curate* in the *Sorcerer.* The *"Bab" Ballads* are filled with clerical characters. Nevertheless, there were clear limitations as to how far fun could go in this direction. In Gilbert's England, even when made topsy-turvy, you must not ridicule the doctrines of the Church; funny verses about the Resurrection or the Holy Communion wouldn't go. But you might laugh all you liked at queer clerical characters and satirize odd clerical usages.

And here a very peculiar distinction had grown up in the current humour of that day. It was not "the thing" to make fun of the Church of England or to ridicule its doctrines. But it was all right to ridicule the doctrines of the Roman Catholic Church. It was all right to laugh at relics and indulgences and pardons because these things were really funny, being superstitions. It was all wrong to laugh at the Holy Communion of the Church of England because this was a sacred mystery. Indeed, at a certain point, such ridicule became blasphemy and the law would deal with it. Even for people who didn't believe much, it was "bad form" to make fun of the Church. But you could have all the jokes you liked about fat friars and drunken abbots and juggling priests and hocus-pocus. Take this for example. It comes in the description of a dinner given in a monastery by the Abbot to the Devil, who had wickedly assumed the deceptive form of a pretty lady visitor:

> She pledged him once and she pledged him twice
> And she drank as lady ought not to drink;
> And he pressed her hand neath the table thrice
> And he winked as Abbot ought not to wink.

> And Peter the Prior and Francis the Friar
> Sat each with a napkin under his chin;
> But Roger the monk got excessively drunk
> So they put him to bed and they tucked him in.

Roaringly funny, isn't it? I am sure that Lewis Carroll, who found it very wicked of Mr. Gilbert to make fun of bishops and curates of the real Church, would have doubled up with laughter over Roger the monk getting excessively drunk. But how would it be if the Archbishop of Canterbury gave the dinner and the Bishop of Ripon was as full as a pippin and the Bishop of Bath was more than half? No, that wouldn't be amusing at all because it would be making fun of men whose sacred calling removes them from all humour. Such was the peculiar way in which the Anglican pot laughed at the Catholic kettle. Indeed, the author of the above verses was himself a clergyman, the Reverend Richard Harris Barham (1788-1845), a man much respected for his piety, his kindly life and his antiquarian knowledge. But when he picked up the pen as Thomas Ingoldsby and wrote the *Ingoldsby Legends*, a book of mingled humorous verse and droll legend, that was very different. He, it was, who wrote the still surviving *Jackdaw of Rheims*, the story of the unhappy bird which stole the cardinal's rye and so encountered the full explosive blast of a curse of the Church of Rome, which knocked all its feathers sideways.

This queer attitude toward "Romanism" was, like the other

things, a survival. The days had gone when people died in the flames at Smithfield for Protestantism; or when Roman Catholic priests were hunted down as criminals, and witches burned with universal approval. But the smouldering ashes were there still, deep down, still are. Hence, even with active persecution gone and practical rights granted by the Catholic Emancipation Act of 1829, it was quite in order to make jokes on Roman Catholic idolatry. It was like kicking a dead dog that might not be quite dead.

With which we can open our *"Bab" Ballads* again and see where we are in regard to the Church of England itself. Here is the Bishop of Rum-ti-Foo, a very merry character, hailing evidently from what were, in Gilbert's day, the Cannibal Isles, but, in ours, sunk far below that. The Bishop amuses his curé of dark souls with conjuring tricks. That was all right and very funny, being only in the Colonies. The Bishop had left his flock and made a visit to London. On his return he was horrified to find that during his absence rough sailors had landed on Rum-ti-Foo and taught the natives all sorts of dreadful profanity such as "bother!" and "blow!" They had reverted to their native Pacific Island dress, or lack of dress:

> Except a shell—a bangle rare—
> A feather here—a feather there—

The Bishop, of course, is greatly concerned and devotes himself with true missionary zeal and self-sacrifice to the redemption of his flock.

> The Bishop's eyes with water fill,
> Quite overjoyed to find them still
> Obedient to his sovereign will,
>   And said, "Good Rum-ti-Foo!
> Half-way I'll meet you, I declare:
> I'll dress myself in cowries rare,
> And fasten feathers in my hair,
>   And dance the 'Cutch-chi-boo!' "

And to conciliate his see
He married Piccadillillee,
The youngest of his twenty-three,
    Tall—neither fat nor thin.
(And though the dress he made her don
Looks awkwardly a girl upon,
It was a great improvement on
    The one he found her in.)

The Bishop in his gay canoe
(His wife, of course, went with him too)
To some adjacent island flew,
    To spend his honeymoon.
Some day in sunny Rum-ti-Foo
A little Peter'll be on view;
And that (if people tell me true)
    Is like to happen soon.

So much for the labours of the Bishop of Rum-ti-Foo. One doubts if it was calculated to advance the cause of missionary enterprise. One may compare it with Dickens' Mrs. Jellyby (in *Bleak House*) and her labours for the natives of Borrioboola-Gha. One may compare it, too, with the grim picture of Somerset Maugham's *Rain* that has gone around the world as story, play, and picture. I rather think I prefer the Bishop of Rum-ti-Foo to anything we have now.

Equally merry on the surface but deeply satirical below is another church picture *The Reverend Simon Magus*. Here the satire is directed only against the usages, not against the doctrines, of the Established Church. It begins:

A rich advowson, highly prized,
    For private sale was advertised;
And many a parson made a bid;
    The Reverend Simon Magus did.

We must pause a moment to explain what an advowson is, or rather was, in Gilbert's time, for the right it carries has been greatly modified by later statutes. It meant the right of "Presentation to a vacant ecclesiastical benefice"; that is, the right, in plainer language, to name (practically to appoint) a clergyman to a particular position fallen vacant. This was a form of property. It originated centuries ago out of various gifts given to the Church which carried a *quid pro quo* or, shall we say, a string on them. The right could be bought or sold, even at auction, and in the case of a rich benefice it carried a high price. It is only fair to admit that the right could not be exercised by a lunatic or a Roman Catholic; still less by a Roman Catholic lunatic. Here the universities of Oxford and Cambridge stepped in and took the place of the lunatic. It is fair, also, to admit that the bishop of the diocese might object to the person presented as not fit to be a clerk in holy orders. In which case the owner of the advowson could come back at him with a writ of *quare impedit* (why is he stopping me?) and the proposed clerk could join in with a *duplex querela*—that means a side kick—and the whole matter drift slowly sideways toward the Court of Chancery. We don't have fun like that in newer countries.

So now one can understand Gilbert's delight in Simon Magus' dickering with an agent for the advowson . . .

> A rich advowson, highly prized,
> For private sale was advertised;
> And many a parson made a bid;
> The Reverend Simon Magus did.
>
> He sought the agent's: "Agent, I
> Have come prepared at once to buy
> (If your demand is not too big)
> The Curé of Otium-cum-Digge."
>
> "Ah!" said the agent, "*there's* a berth—
> The snuggest vicarage on earth;
> No sort of duty (so I hear),
> And fifteen hundred pounds a year!

"If on the price we should agree,
The living soon will vacant be;
The good incumbent's ninety-five,
And cannot very long survive.

"See—here's his photograph—you see,
He's in his dotage." "Ah, dear me!
Poor soul!" said Simon. "His decease
Would be a merciful release!"

The agent laughed—the agent blinked—
The agent blew his nose and winked—
And poked the parson's ribs in play—
It was that agent's vulgar way.

The Reverend Simon frowned: "I grieve
This light demeanour to perceive;
It's scarcely *comme il faut*, I think:
Now—pray oblige me—do not wink.

"Don't dig my waistcoat into holes—
Your mission is to sell the souls
Of human sheep and human kids
To that divine who highest bids.

"Do well in this, and on your head
Unnumbered honours will be shed."
The agent said, "Well, truth to tell,
I *have* been doing very well."

"You should," said Simon, "at your age;
But now about the parsonage.
How many rooms does it contain?
Show me the photograph again.

A poor apostle's humble house
Must not be too luxurious;
No stately halls with oaken floor—
It should be decent and no more.

"No billiard-rooms—no stately trees—
No croquet-grounds or pineries."

"Ah!" sighed the agent, "very true:
This property won't do for you.

"All these about the house you'll find"—
"Well," said the parson, "never mind;
I'll manage to submit to these
Luxurious superfluities.

"A clergyman who does not shirk
The various calls of Christian work
Will have no leisure to employ
These 'common forms' of worldly joy.

"To preach three times on Sabbath days—
To wean the lost from wicked ways—
The sick to soothe—the sane to wed—
The poor to feed with meat and bread;

"These are the various wholesome ways
In which I'll spend my nights and days:
My zeal will have no time to cool
At croquet, archery, or pool."

The agent said, "From what I hear,
This living will not suit, I fear—
There are no poor, no sick at all;
For services there is no call."

The reverend gent looked grave. "Dear me!
Then there is *no* 'society'?—
I mean, of course, no sinners there
Whose souls will be my special care?"

The cunning agent shook his head,
"No, none—except"—(the agent said)—
"The Duke of A., the Earl of B.,
The Marquis C., and Viscount D.

"But you will not be quite alone,
For, though they've chaplains of their own,
Of course this noble well-bred clan
Receive the parish clergyman."

"Oh, silence, sir!" said Simon M.,
"Dukes—earls! What should I care for them?
These worldly ranks I scorn and flout,
Of course." The agent said, "No doubt."

"Yet I might show these men of birth
The hollowness of rank on earth."
The agent answered, "Very true—
But I should not, if I were you."

"Who sells this rich advowson, pray?"
The agent winked—it was his way—
"His name is Hart; twixt me and you,
He is, I'm grieved to say, a Jew!"

"A Jew?" said Simon, "happy find!
I purchase this advowson, mind.
My life shall be devoted to
Converting that unhappy Jew."

But observe how different is the treatment of the Roman Catholic Church. All of its doctrines, except where they are identical with those of the Established Church of England, are a fair mark for ridicule. Nothing is too sacred, not even the confessional and the forgiveness of sins. Take as evidence the Ballad of *Gentle Alice Brown,* in which Gentle Alice confesses her sins to Father Paul and receives an easy absolution.

It was a robber's daughter, and her name was Alice Brown,
Her father was the terror of a small Italian town;
Her mother was a foolish, weak, but amiable old thing;
But it isn't of her parents that I'm going for to sing.

As Alice was a-sitting at her window-sill one day,
A beautiful young gentleman he chanced to pass that way;
She cast her eyes upon him, and he looked so good and true,
That she thought, "I could be happy with a gentleman like you!"

And every morning passed her house that cream of gentlemen,
She knew she might expect him at a quarter unto ten;

A sorter in the Custom-house, it was his daily road
(The Custom-house was fifteen minutes' walk from her abode).

But Alice was a pious girl, who knew it wasn't wise
To look at strange young sorters with expressive purple eyes;
So she sought the village priest to whom her family confessed,
The priest by whom their little sins were carefully assessed.

"Oh, holy father," Alice said, " 'twould grieve you, would it not,
To discover that I was a most disreputable lot?
Of all unhappy sinners I'm the most unhappy one!"
The padre said, "Whatever have you been and gone and done?"

"I have helped mama to steal a little kiddy from its dad,
I've assisted dear papa in cutting up a little lad,
I've planned a little burglary and forged a little cheque,
And slain a little baby for the coral on its neck!"

The worthy pastor heaved a sigh, and dropped a silent tear,
And said, "You mustn't judge yourself too heavily, my dear:
"It's wrong to murder babies, little corals for to fleece;
But sins like these one expiates at half-a-crown apiece."

"Girls will be girls—you're very young, and flighty in your mind;
Old heads upon young shoulders we must not expect to find,
We mustn't be too hard upon these little girlish tricks.
Let's see—five crimes at half-a-crown—exactly twelve and six."

But Alice now confesses to her improper conduct in connection with the young sorter. Father Paul is, of course, horrified at the idea of the robber's daughter falling in love outside of the bandit class into respectable society. That kind of thing would mean the end of crime and confessional fees. However, it all ends happily. Father Paul communicates at once with Robber Brown who goes after the young sorter without delay.

He traced that gallant sorter to a still suburban square;
He watched his opportunity and seized him unaware;
He took a life-preserver and he hit him on the head,
And Mrs. Brown dissected him before she went to bed.

Observe the last line.

Mrs. Brown dissected him before she went to bed.

This is another example of that apparently open "brutality" which offended Mark Lemon when the *Nancy Bell's* cook was tipped into the pot, boiled and eaten! Here we have Mrs. Brown, sitting quietly at her dissection, carefully separating the *os femoris* from the *patella*, and laying aside the articular cartilege for later disposal. This sounds very horrible if you really think of it. But the point is you don't think about it. We have a sort of compartment in our minds, evoluted for our protection, to keep actuality and fun apart. I admit that if you push too hard on the partition it will give way. The boiling of the cook is at too high pressure for most of us. I remember, also, the story of a funeral of a locomotive engineer who had been scalded to death. The clergyman spoke of him to the mourners as "our 'steemed friend." That, I always found a little bit thick—with steam.

But good Mrs. Brown and her dissection may pass for another reason; namely, the excellence of the phrase, "before she went to bed." The *"Bab" Ballads* and the Gilbert and Sullivan operas are filled with those happy phrases which people loved to quote, though probably few people could explain just exactly why. The point here is the beautiful domesticity of the phrase. It belongs in family life. It suggests one of those domestic tasks which no good housewife likes to leave undone over night. She always gets all her dishes washed and her kitchen tidy every night. And so good Mrs. Brown felt that she must get her dissecting done "before she went to bed."

Probably many people will agree that the most sustained effort, the most finished satire and the most exquisite flow of verse in the *"Bab" Ballads* is found in the poem *Etiquette*. This was not one of the original ballads of *Fun*. It was written years later for a Christmas number of the *Graphic*. But Gilbert himself gathered it into the large volume of early ballads and later songs which he collected in 1897 as the *"Bab" Ballads, etc.*

I was about to say that here, at any rate, we have a poem with none of those disfiguring details of horror of which we have just spoken. But I notice on looking again that the poem starts off with the wholesale drowning of an entire ship's company, including the owners. Still, that's nothing. It's not the point of the poem and, as Gilbert himself says, they were all insured.

The underlying satire of the poem turns on the aloofness of English manners, the impossibility of knowing anybody that you don't know. But its great merit lies in the smooth perfection of its lines, which seem so effortless and so inevitable, the last word in comic verse.

Date Due

Printed in P.E.I. by Island Offset Inc.